J. M. Nallaswami Pillai

Sivagnana Botham Of Meykanda Deva

J. M. Nallaswami Pillai

Sivagnana Botham Of Meykanda Deva

ISBN/EAN: 9783744643443

Printed in Europe, USA, Canada, Australia, Japan

Cover: Foto ©Lupo / pixelio.de

More available books at **www.hansebooks.com**

SIVAGNANA BOTHAM

OF

MEYKANDA DEVA

TRANSLATED WITH NOTES AND INTRODUCTION

BY

J. M. NALLASWAMI PILLAI, B. A., B. L.,

District Munsiff.

1895

Sivagnana Botham of Meykanda Deva

PREFACE

(1895 Edition)

A few words will suffice to introduce the book to the public. The original work is regarded as the Muthal Nul, Revealed book fo the Saiva Religion and Siddhanta Philosophy. When I first began the translation, I was rather diffident about the sort of reception it will meet with in the hands of the public; but, since, I have been able to discuss some of the subjects herein contained with many intelligent persons, belonging to all shades of opinion, Hindu and Christian and all of them have spoken appreciatively of the work. I have also received assurances from several valued friends about the importance of the work. Besides, from the facts I set out below, I am led to believe that the time of appearance of this book is quite opportune. Within the last two or three weeks I have come across three important publications, which have prepared the public mind, here and in England, for an appreciative study of the Tamil, Moral, Religious and Philosophical writings. I refer to the Rev. Doctor G. U. Pope's paper on 'Ethics of Modern Hinduism', Professor P. Sundaram Pillai's 'some milestones in the History of Tamil Literature' or 'The age of Tirugnana Sambantha' and the recent article of the Rev. G. M. Cobban in the Contemporary Review, entitled 'Latent Religion of India'. Of these, 'Some milestone' contain an elaborate critical resume of the History of the Saiva Literature in Tamil from the 5th century down to the 13th century; and the other contributions contain a review of the Saiva Ethics and Religion and Philosophy of about the same period. Doctor Pope in referring to the Tamil Kural observes, "In this great and ancient language, there exists among much else, that is interesting and valuable, an ethical treatise, not surpassed (as far as I know) by anything of the kind in any literature". And in pages 3 and 4 of his paper, he discusses the Siddhanta doctrine of the three Padarthas, Pathi, Pasu and Pasa, on which this Ethics is based. And in the end, the Rev. Doctor is forced to confess, even after making all sorts of reservations and qualifications that "it is evident from what has been said above, we have in Southern India, the outlines at least of a doctrine of ethics, which in a Christian point of view is nearly unexceptionable". And he is good enough to add, 'to meet thoughtful Hindus in a spirit of dogmatic antagonism, or to treat them with contempt or to speak of them as the perishing heathen is absolutely unfitting. We have even something to learn from Hinduism'. But the deeply implanted prejudice lingers, and it leads him to say that truth found in the Kural must have been derived from a Christian source. The Rev. G. M. Cobban is more generous in this respect. He says, "First I think we should insist on the cordial recognition of these truths, and cheerfully acknowledge their kinship to Christianity, for all truth is akin. The Hindu poet knows what to say of it. He says 'the heart is made pure by the truth'. If I am asked whence these truths came, I would say from Heaven, from Him who is the Truth. But, whether they are the direct gifts of God to the Hindus, or whether as boulders, they have drifted and have travelled to India, I cannot tell; the evidence on this point is incomplete. If any urge that, although Hindus recognize their authority, they are uninspired, and not really authoritative, I would say truth is authoritative, because it is truth, not because it came in a particular way. And all truth is from God". The Siddhantis not only believe that 'the heart is made pure by truth', but that no truth should be thought as faulty, even if it is found in an alien book.

Sivagnana Botham of Meykanda Deva

"அந்நிய நூலின் விதி யவிரோதமேல்
உன்னேல் பழுதென்றுளத்து"

The article in question, after reviewing briefly the attitude of Missionaries towards Hinduism from time to time proceeds to state, "we find much truth both in books and men; so Christian teacher". The article gives a brief summary of the Siddhanta doctrines and quotations from nearly all the Siddhanta Sastras and other works referred to by me in the body of the work. After these quotations, follow a remark, "If we give to the truths enumerated and illustrated above, our careful consideration, we shall admit that they indicate a clear advance on the teaching of the Vedas or the Pantheism of the Upanishads". But that is an issue raised between Siddhantis and other Vedantists as to what the Vedas and Upanishads really teach, which I explain further in my introduction. I am afraid that Hinduism has lost more than what it has gained by an one-sided representation from within and from without; by translating and publishing such works and interpretations only as accord with the Idealistic School of Hindu Philosophy. No doubt the truth is here, but not in the latent condition as the Rev. Gentleman supposes. This is the truth which has been taught to me and which I have learned from my earliest years; and neither my parents nor my teachers have ever taught me to mistake a stock or a stone for God. The truth is here and it is not kept concealed as is supposed; and the words have gone forth, thrice,

1) "* * * ஒன்றாய்ப் பலவாய் வுயிர்க்குயிராய்,
ஆடுங்கருணைப் பரஞ்சோதி யருளைப் பெறுதற்கு அன்புநிலை,
தேடும் பருவமிது கண்டீர் சேரவாரும் சகத்தீரே."

(2) "பொய்வந் துழலும் சமயநெறி புகுத வேண்டாம் முத்திதரும்
தெய்வ சபையைக் காண்பதற்குச் சேரவாரும் சகத்தீரே."

(3) "* * * அகண்டாகாரசிவ போக மெனும் பேரின்ப வெள்ளம் பொங்கிக்
ததும்பிப் பூரணமாய்,
ஏகவுருவாய்க் கிடக்குதையோ, வின்புற்றிட நாமெடுத்த
தேகம் விழுமுன் புசிப்பதற்குச் சேரவாரும் சகத்தீரே."

and let them who have ears to hear, hear.

(1) O! Come Ye together from all parts of this world! See, this is the time for finding that condition of Love which will secure us the Arul (Grace) of that Gracious, and Supreme Light, which is One, which is All, and which is the Life of life.

(2) O! Come Ye together, to see the Divine Presence, which will give Moksha; and don't enter the paths of those religions which wallow in untruth.

(3) Oh! That Great Flood of Joy of Limitless Sivabhoga is rising and flowing over; and It is filling everything and yet remains One! Come Ye together to partake of It, and obtain bliss, before ever our bodies perish!

Sivagnana Botham of Meykanda Deva

The worst feature of modern Hinduism is pointed out to be its idolatry; and the Rev. Gentleman would persist in calling it the substitute for truth and not truth's symbol. I have discussed the pros and cons of this question in my notes to the Sixth Sutra; and so much prejudice and ignorance prevail in regard to this question, that all that I would crave for, is a fair and patient hearing. I refer the reader also to an excellent Tamil book brought out by Sri la Sri Somasundara Nayagar Avergal of Madras entitled 'Archadipam' in which this question is also more fully treated.

Before concluding, I cannot resist the temptation of indulging in one more extract from the valuable article of the Rev. G. M. Cobban, the appropriateness of which the readers will easily perceive.

"I once spent a few days with a fakir on his way to Rameswaram as a pilgrim. We travelled together and having come to be friends, he told me how he had spent four years in the jungle as the disciple of a celebrated religious teacher (Guru) and Saint. 'And what did he teach you during your first year,' I asked. 'The Sacredness of truth,' was the reply. 'How did he teach it?' By teaching me nothing during the year. He was testing me to see if I was worthy to receive the truth.' 'And what did he teach you in the succeeding years.' 'He spoke to me seldom, and taught me in all twelve Sanskrit Slokas.' (24 lines). The instruments of the disciple's culture were few and simple, and its area small. Half a page of Sanskrit does not seem an exhaustive College Course. But the slokas stretched to infinity as the student gazed on them with the inner eye, and in a narrow space, and on the strong food of this small curriculum, he had grown to be an acute and strong thinker. But had he failed to show himself worthy to receive the truth, the Guru would not have taught him."

The twelve slokas, the Hindu fakir referred to may or may not be the twelve Sutras of Sivagnanabotha, but nevertheless, the above remarks are equally appropriate.

Compare the words of Thayumanavar in praise of the author of Sivagnana Siddhi,

"பாதிவிருத் தத்தாலிப் பார்விருத்த மாகவுண்மை,
சாதித்தார் பொன்னடியைத் தான் பணிவ தெந்நாளோ,"

"O for the day! when I can worship the golden feet of him who declared the truth, in half a stanza by which I lost all my illusions."

In conclusion, I have to tender my thanks to Pandit Murugesam Pillai Avergal, who assisted me in my study of the Tamil Commentaries and to M. R. Ry. Tandalam Balasundaram Mudaliar Avergal, who rendered invaluable help by his suggestions etc., while these sheets were passing through the Press and to Messrs. G. Ramaswamy Chetty & Co., who have displayed very great care and taste in the get up of the book.

TRIPATUR,   J. M. N
6th July, 1895.

Sivagnana Botham of Meykanda Deva

TABLE OF CONTENTS

	Page No.
Introduction	6
Note on the Author	12
List of Agamas	17
List of Siddhanta works in Tamil	17
Sivagnanabotha Sutra in Devanagiri	18
Sivagnanabotha Sutra in Tamil	19
Sivagnanabotha Sutra in English	21
Invocation to Ganesha	23
Author' Apology	24

Chapter I: - Pramanaviyal or Proof
First Sutra.	On the Existence of God	25
Second Sutra.	The relation of God to the world and to the souls	31
Third Sutra.	On the Existence of the Soul	44

Chapter II: - Lakshanavial
Fourth Sutra.	Of the Soul in its relation to the Andhakarana	50
Fifth Sutra.	On the relation of God, Soul and body	56
Sixth Sutra.	On the nature of God and the world	59

Chapter III: - Sathanavial
Seventh Sutra.	Respecting the Soul	69
Eight Sutra.	The way in which Souls obtain Wisdom	73
Ninth Sutra.	On the purification of the Soul	78

Chapter IV: - Payanial
Tenth Sutra: -	The way of destroying Pasa	81
Eleventh Suta: -	The way by which the Soul unites with God	85
Twelfth Sutra: -	On the mode of worship of God who surpasses Powers of Thought and Speech	89

In Praise of Meikanda Deva	93
Glossary of Sanskrit and Tamil words	94

Sivagnana Botham of Meykanda Deva

INTRODUCTION

The system of Hindu Philosophy which is expounded in the following pages, and its name will be altogether new to many an English educated Hindu who is content to learn his religion and philosophy from English books and translations and from such scraps as turn up in newspapers and magazines and from such scraps as turn up in newspapers and magazines. Yet it is the Philosophy of the Religion in which at least every Tamil speaking Hindu is more or less brought up and the one Philosophy which obtains predominance in the Tamil Languages. This Philosophy is called The **Siddhanta Philosophy** and is the special Philosophy of the Saiva Religion. The word means True End, and as used in logic, it means the proposition or theory proved as distinguished from the proposition or theory refuted, which becomes the **Purvapaksham**. The Saiva Philosophy is so called as it establishes the True End or the only Truth and all other systems are merely **Purvapakshams**. The system is based primarily on the **Saiva Agamas**. But the authority of the **Vedas** is equally accepted and the system is then called **Vedanta Philosophy** or **Vedanta Siddhantha Philosophy** or **Vaithika Saiva Philosophy**.

"வேதாந்த சித்தாந்த சமரச நன்னிலை பெற்ற,
வித்தகச் சித்தர் கணமே."
"ராஜாங்கத்தில் அமர்ந்தது வைதிக சைவ மழகிதந்தோ."

(Thayumanavar). This Philosophy is also spoken of as **Adwaitha Philosophy** in all the Tamil works and it will be seen from the very large use of the word and its exposition in almost every page of this work what important part it plays; and it strikes, in fact, the key not of the whole system. **Meikanda Devar** who translated and commented on **Sivagnana Botham** is called "**Adwaitha Meikandan**" அத்துவித மெய்கண்டான், one who saw the **Truth of Adwaitha**) by Thayumanavar. However, it is the **Agama** which gives the Philosophy its form and language. Very absurd notions are entertained of the **Agamas** or **Tantras**, specially derived from the low practices of the Right-hand followers or Vamabahinis of Bengal and proceeding from ignorance of the real works, through want of published books and translations. The books followed by the Left-hand Section or South Indian Sects are altogether different and I give a list of them below. Very little notice is taken of them by Oriental Scholars and of the existing works the **Karma Kanda** are alone preserved to us. There are several of these works in the great Mutt at Thiruvavaduthurai; and an excellent commentary on one of the **Upagamas**, **Paushkara**, by Umapathi Sivacharya is also preserved there. Like the **Veda** or **Mantra**, the **Agama** or **Tantra** is divided into **Karma Kanda** and **Gnana Kanda** and there were a large number of **Upagamas** corresponding to Upanishads, of which **Mrigendra** is very largely quoted by Sayanacharya in his Sarvadarsana Sangraha. The true relation of the **Agama** to the **Veda** is pointed out by Swami Vivekananda in his address to the Madras people and I quote his observations below. "The **Tantras** as we have said, represent the 'Vedic rituals' in a modified form, and before any one jumps into the most absurd conclusions about them, I will advise him to read the **Tantras** in connection with the 'Brahmanas' especially of the 'Adhwarya' portion. And most of the '**Mantras**' used in the '**Tantras**' will be found taken

Sivagnana Botham of Meykanda Deva

verbatim from these 'Brahmanas.' As to their influence, apart from the '**Srouta**' and '**Smarta**' rituals, all other forms of ritual observed from the Himalayas to the Comorin have been taken from the 'Tantras' and they direct the worship of the Saktas, the Saivas, the Vaishnavas and all others alike."

I am also informed that the sources of the rules for the rituals followed by Smartas and which are now taken from some manuals and compilations of very recent origin are really found in the **Agamas** or **Tantras**. However, the **Agamas** are held in very high repute by the Non-Smartha populations of Southern India; and the **Agama** is as much held to be the word of the Deity as the **Veda**, the word literally meaning "The Revealed Word."

Says Saint Thirumular: -

"வேதமொடு ஆகமம் மெய்யாம் இறைவனூல்
ஓதும் பொதுவும் சிறப்புமென் றுன்னுக
நாதன் உரையிவை நாடில் இரண்டந்தம்
பேதம் தென்னில் பெரியோர்க் கபேதமே.·

"The Vedas and Agamas are both of them true, both being the word of the Lord. Think that the first is a general treatise and the latter a special one. Both form the word of God. When examined, and where difference is perceived between Vedanta and Siddhanta, the great will perceive no such difference."

Says Sri Nilakanta Charya: -

"Vayanthu Vedasivagamayorbhedam,
Napasyamaha Vedopisivagamaha."

(I don't perceive any difference between the **Veda** and the **Sivagama**. The **Veda** itself is the **Sivagama**.)

It is needless to observe that **Sri Nilakanta** or **Sri Kanta Charya** belongs to the Saiva School; and it is no less surprising to see so little notice taken of him and his works by Oriental Scholars in their general account of Hindu Religious and Philosophies. And strange it is that even the learned Swami whom I have quoted above does not mention his name, though he mentions **Sri Sankara, Sri Ramanuja** and **Sri Madvacharya** and a host of other names small and great. Sri Kanta was a friend and contemporary of Govinda Yogi, the Guru of Sri Sankara and his **Bhashya** of **Vyasa Sariraka Sutras** according to most accounts was anterior to that of Sri Sankara's Bashya itself. And though he does not call his **Vedanta Bashya** as such, it is popularly known as **Visishtadwaitha Bashya** or **Sutta Adwaita Bashya**. And the work is published in parts in the Pandit Vols. 6 and 7. This commentary of **Sri Kanta Charya**, the learned translator of the **Vedanta Sutras**, Mr. George Thibaut does not seem to have come across, and he nowhere alludes to it by name; and yet the results arrived at by him as to the teachings of the Sutras after a lengthy discussion and comparison of the respective interpretations of the texts by **Sri Sankara** and **Sri Ramanuja**, exactly fall in with the interpretation of the Sutras by **Sri Kanta Charya**. The learned translator observes

Sivagnana Botham of Meykanda Deva

(Introduction p. c.) "If, now, I am shortly to sum up the results of the preceding enquiry, as to the teaching of the sutras, I must give it as my opinion that they do not set forth the distinction of a higher and lower knowledge of Brahman; that they do not acknowledge the distinction of Brahman and Isvara in Sankara's sense; that they do not hold the doctrine of the unreality of the world; that they do not, with Sankara, proclaim the absolute identity of the individual and the highest self." These are exactly points where **Sankara** and **Sri Kanta** differ. The translator further remarks that he agrees with **Ramanuja's** mode of interpretation in some important details, for instance, in regard to the doctrine of **Parinama Vada** and interpretation of fourth **Adhyaya**. These are also points where **Ramanuja** agrees with **Sri Kanta**. But Sri Kanta differs from both in their interpretations of the passages referring to **Nirguna** and **Saguna Brahm**, and follows the doctrine of the Siddhantha School. And the doctrine of **Parinama Vada** is the only distinguishing mark of **Sri Kanta's Vedanta Philosophy** as opposed to the **Siddhantha Philosophy**; and it is this **Vedanta** and not **Sankara's Vedanta**, that is referred to approvingly by all Tamil writers and Sagas, as in the passage of **Thirumular** and **Thayumanavar** above quoted. The ground work of **Sivagnana Botham** is the one adopted by **Sri Kanta** for the **Vedanta Sutras**, and as far as I have been able to compare, they exactly tally, except where **Sankara's** forced explanations enter; and the passages will certainly lose their meaning unless it is viewed in its proper place, as for instance, in regard to the purport of the 2nd Sutra of the first **Adhyaya**, the objection of the translator (p. xcii) which is perfectly cogent, will lose its point, if it is not taken as a definition of God but as involving the proof of the existence of God. The Sutra, "Brahman is that whence the origination and so on (i. e. the sustentation and reabsorption) of this world proceed," is exactly the same as the first Sutra of **Sivagnana Botham** and the same meaning is conveyed by the first **Kural** of **Thiruvalluvar** also. In passing, I may refer the render to the **Swetaswatara Upanishad**, translated by Dr. Roer, the philosophy of which is exactly the same as herein expounded, though the learned doctor puzzles himself as to what this philosophy could be which is neither **Vedanta**, nor **Sankhya** nor **Yoga** and yet reconciles or attempts to reconcile all these doctrines.

Coming back to the **Agamas**, very little is known regarding its antiquity from the point of view of the European Scholar. The **Nyayikas** use the word **Agama Pramana**, where we would now say **Sruti Pramana**, meaning Revealed Word, the word of God or of the highest authority. So, that the **Agamas** should go back for behind their time. As the popular phrase runs, **Vedagama Purana Itikasa Smrities**, its period should be fixed after the Vedas and before the rest of the group. Observes Rev. Hoisington, the first translator into English of **Sivagnana Botham**, "the Agamam which contains the doctrinal treatise given in this work, may safely be ascribed to what I would term the Philosophical Period of Hinduism, the period between the **Vedic** and **Puranic** Eras. These doctrines can be traced in the earlier works of the **Puranic** period, in the **Ramayana**, the **Bhagavat Gita**, and the **Manava Dharma Sastra**. They are so alluded to and involved in those works, as to evince that they were already systematized and established. We have the evidence or some Tamil works that the **Agama** doctrines were revived in the south of India before Brahminism by which I mean Mythological Hinduism obtained any prominent place there. From some statements in the **Ramayana**, it would appear that they were adopted in the South before Rama's time. This would fix their date at more than a thousand years before the Christian Era, certainly as early as that of the

Sivagnana Botham of Meykanda Deva

Ramayanam." Adopting another method, it can be very easily shown that they go far behind the date of Buddha, and though it is said that the religion of the Hindus at that time was Hinduism (a meaningless word from the stand point of the Hindu) the only religion which stood against Buddhism and Jainism in their palmist days and into which they finally merged themselves, without leaving a single vestige in India, was the Saiva Religion. The struggles between Buddhism and Jainism and Saivaism are celebrated in the annals of our saints, **Upamanya Bhakta Vilasa** and the Tamil **Peria Purana**, and of these saints the great Manickavachaka, the famous author of **Thiruvachakam** belonged to the Buddhist period and the great **Gnana Sambantha** and **Vakisa**, the authors of '**Thevaram**,' belonged to the Jain period, though our learned Swami Vivekananda seems to know very little of them, in spite of the fact that all our temples in Southern India and not a few in the utmost bounds of Mysore Province contain their images and all the principal festivals in Madras and in the mofussil are celebrated in their honor, I refer to the Makiladi feast in Thiruvottiyur, Aruvathumuvar feast in Mylapore, Aruthra feast in Chidambaram and Avanimula feast in Madura, not to speak of innumerable other feasts connected with every other temple. Such is the paucity of knowledge possessed by foreigners and conveyed in the English language regarding south Indian Chronology, language, religion and Philosophy, chiefly through want of patriotism and enthusiasm on the part of Tamil speaking Indians of the South. Regarding the antiquity of the Saiva Religion itself, M. Barth after observing that the genesis of the Religion is involved in extreme obscurity says that "the Vedic writings chance upon them and as it were go along side of them, during the very period of their formation."

Of course, the difficulty will appear to those who study these writings and the Philosophy contained in them apart from the Religion and Religious beliefs of the people and the religion and beliefs of the people apart from the writings and the Philosophy contained therein, and the difficulty will certainly vanish when the two are studied together and it is perceived how intimately the two are connected together and how the one enters into the very whoof and warp of the other. Coming now to the work in question, the twelve **Sanskrit Sutras** in **Anushtup** metre form part of **Rourava Agama** and have been separately styled and handed down as '**Sivagnana Botham**.' The Saivas believe that this is the very book which was in the hands of the **Divine Guru, Dhakshanamurthi** and these were the very doctrines which He taught to the Great Vedic Rishis, Sanaka, Sanathara, Sanantana and Sanatkumara. At any rate, as an example of such close and condensed reasoning, embracing as it does the whole of the field of Religion and Philosophy, the work is unparalleled. The Sariraka Sutras of Vyasa, which contain the same four divisions as the present work, consist of 555 sutras. There can be no doubt that the Tamilians, having very early secured a translation of this work through Meikanda Deva with his invaluable commentary, cared to possess no translation of any other work on Philosophy from the Sanskrit, and in spite of the great praise that is bestowed on the Bhagavat Gita, the Tamil reader knows nothing about it, and it is only recently a Tamil translation has been got out. Of the merits of this Philosophy, which is discussed here as the **Adwaitha Philosophy**, the word **Visishtadwaitha** having never come into use with the Tamil writers, I need say nothing here following the example of the first translator Rev. H. R. Hoisington who neither says a word in blame nor in praise of it, leaving the readers themselves to form their opinions. It is more than 40 years since he published his translation of this work and of two

Sivagnana Botham of Meykanda Deva

other works in the Journal of the American Oriental Society, Vol. No. IV. And I am not in a position to know what criticism it elicited then. Probably it was shelved as offering no points of attack. The objections usually taken by Missionaries and Oriental Scholars against Vedantism fall flat if urged against this theory, as herein expounded. Of the Rev. H. R. Hoisington and his translation, I must say a few words. He was an American Missionary attached to the Batticotta Seminary in Ceylon. He came to know of the work early and it is almost pathetic now to read after 40 years, what difficulties he had to contend with, before he was able to master the subject and complete the translation and no meed of praise is sufficient for this and other disinterested seekers after the truth, wherever it may be found. Nor are these difficulties even vanished to-day. Consequent on the extreme terseness of diction and brevity of expression employed in the work, even the ordinary Pundits are not able to understand without proper commentaries; and very few Pundits could be found in Southern India who are able to expound the text properly even now. For several years, it was in my thoughts to attempt a translation of this work, and time and place not permitting, I was only able to begin it about the middle of last year and when I had fairly begun my translation, I learnt from a note in Trubner's **Sarva Darsana Sangraha** that a previous translation of this work existed and hunting out for this book, I chanced upon an old catalogue of Bishop Caldwell and I subsequently traced out the possession of Bishop Caldwell's book to Rev. J. Lazarus, B. A., of Madras who very courteously lent me the use of the book and to whom my best thanks are due. I have used the book to see that I do not go wrong in essential points and in the language of the translation. Rev. Hoisington's translation is not literal and is very free and was evidently made from a very free paraphrase given of the text by the pundits. I do not find anything corresponding to the Varthika commentary of Meikanda Deva in his translation; and in the elucidation of the text and original commentary, I have followed the excellent commentary of Sivagnana Yogi, which I think was not available to Mr. Hoisington, in print then. I must say here that it gave me very great encouragement and pleasure to proceed in the task to hear from a well-known Professor of the South, who wrote to say, "It gives me very great pleasure that the Saiva Siddhanta Philosophy is after all, to be written in English. I should myself have undertaken the work gladly, if my health had permitted the task. As it is, I am happy you have found time to undertake the difficult though laudable task of translating into English, the Philosophic teachings of our Siddhanta Sastras."

I hope the notes which I have added will be found of use to the ordinary reader in understanding the text and I have also added a Glossary of most Sanskrit names and words used in the work. Contrary to the usual practice I have indulged in Tamil quotations, for which, I hope the reader will excuse me. I have largely drawn on 'Thayumanavar,' for the simple reason that he is read by all alike and there is no one in Southern India who does not know him. It is also my object to show how the Philosophy herein expounded has passed into the current thought of the people and their common language, for it might be taken as true that no religion of Philosophy is entitled to be called a living one which does not enter into the common thought of the people and their language. I may also say that my explanation of the text has the full approval of several Orthodox Pundits, of whom I can mention Sri la Sri S. Somasundara Nayagar of Madras, to whom I am largely indebted by means of his lectures and books and pamphlets, for the little knowledge of Saiva religion and Philosophy which I may possess. Of

Sivagnana Botham of Meykanda Deva

course, I must not omit to mention my obligations to Brahma Sri Mathakandana Venkatagiri Sastrigal, the great Saivite Preacher of Malabar who is a Siddhanthin and a follower of Sri Kanta Charya.

His Holiness The Pandara Sannadhigal of Thiruvavaduthorai Mutt and His Holiness, Rai Bahadur, Thirugnana Sambantha Pandara Sannadhigal of Madura Mutt have also been pleased to go through portions of the work and to express their great satisfaction.

In the next note, I will refer briefly to the life of Meikanda Devar who translated the Sutras into Tamil and added his commentary to it and that of some of his followers and commentators.

Sivagnana Botham of Meykanda Deva

NOTE ON THE AUTHOR

"He who translated and commented on Sivagnana Botham, whose knowledge was imparted by Nandi and his disciples, for the purpose of obtaining Salvation, by pointing out the way to proceed from the knowledge of the body full of sorrow, to the knowledge of the soul, and thence to the knowledge of the Supreme Spirit, enshrined in the Maha Vakya, just as the glorious sun, enables our sight by dispelling the deep darkness from the vast surface of this earth;

"He, who under the name of Swethavana lived in Thiruvennainallur, surrounded by the waters of the Pennar;

"He, who left all false knowledge knowing it to be such and was therefore called Meikanda Deva;

"He is the Lord whose feet form the flower worn on the heads of even the holiest sages."

Such is the brief **Sirappu Payiram** which is usually affixed to the Tamil edition of the book, giving particulars of the name and place of the author and the merit of his work.

The author who translated in Tamil, Sivagnana Botham and commented on it was called in early life Swethavana and after he attained spiritual eminence was called Meikanda Deva (meaning Truth finder) and he lived in Thiruvennainallur situated on the banks of the lower Pennar, about 20 miles from Panruti on the S. I. R. line. To this brief account tradition adds the following particulars. One Atchuthan of Pennagadam Village near Thiruvenkadu or Swethavana in Tanjore District, was long childless and he prayed incessantly to Swethavana Ishwara for the boon of a child. One morning he went early to the temple tank and bathed in the tank and when he got up finishing his prayers, he discovered lying on the steps of the tank a new born babe whom he at once pressed to his bosom, and praising God for his mercy to him, took it home and gave it to his wife. And these two were bringing it up. Being the gift of Swethavana Ishwara, the child was named **Swethavana**. In course of time, however, his caste people began to murmur against Atchutha, saying that he is bringing up a low born foundling. The parents were in very deep sorrow on this account, and when Atchuthan's brother-in-law had come to him on a visit from Thiruvennainallur and he offered to take the boy with him and bring him up, they gladly consented and the babe's home became Thiruvennainallur from its 3rd year. It happened, however, that the child was dumb from its birth, but the bent of its mind was discovered in its very play which consisted in making Sivalingam of sand and becoming absorbed in its contemplation. One day, a Siddha, a Jivan Mukta, passing by that way, saw the child in its play and was at once attracted towards it, and observing the child's advanced spiritual condition, he touched it with Grace, altered its name to that of Meikanda Deva, and instructed the child with the Divine Philosophy contained in Sivagnana Botham, and ordered it to translate the same in Tamil and let the world know its truth. The sage, however, retained his silence till his fifth year was past, during which interval it is stated he was receiving further instruction from God Ganesha of Thiruvennainallur, who was called Polla Pillayar, and the abstract of the Sutrams and the various arguments called Churnika is said to have been imparted

Sivagnana Botham of Meykanda Deva

to Meikanda Deva by Polla Pillayar. However, after his fifth year, he began to speak out and preach his Sivagnana Botham and he attracted a very large body of disciples. In those days, there lived in Thiruthoraiyur, a famous pundit and Philosopher named Arulnanthi Sivachariar, well versed in all the Vedas and Agamas, and hence called Sakalagama Pundit. He, with his disciples, came on a visit to Thiruvennainallur; and while there, his disciples became attracted by the teaching of Meikanda Deva and gradually began to desert their former teacher. Arulnanthi Sivachariar came to know of the cause of the desertion of his pupils and went to meet and vanquish Meikanda Deva, face to face. He went there, and the moment the eye of Grace of Meikanda Deva fell on him, he felt his **Ahankara** or **Agnana** leave him and feeling vanquished fell at his feet and sought his grace and from thence became his most prominent and devoted disciple. Here a fact has to be noted. Meikanda Deva was a Vellalah; at least his foster parents were so, and yet Arulnanthi Sivachariar occupying the highest position even among Brahmans did not scruple to become his disciple. Under Meikanda Deva's inspiration Arulnanthi Sivachariar composed a philosophical treatise called **Irupa Irupakthu** (இருபா இருபஃது). Under his direction again, Arulnanthi Sivachariar composed Sivagnana Siddhi, as an authorized commentary on Sivagnana Botham, two works which have been rarely paralleled even in Sanskrit. If the genius of Thiruvalluvar gave to the Tamil language all the teachings to be found in the Vedas, Agamas, Upanishads and Dharma Sastras, on the first three **Purusharthams, Dharma, Artha** and **Kamia** or **Aram, Porul** and **Inbam**, in a thoroughly systematized form, the genius of **Meikanda Deva** and **Arulnanthi Sivacharyar** gave to the Tamil language, all the teachings of these books on the last **Purushartha** namely, **Moksha** or **Veedu**, in a similarly condensed and systematized form. The plan of the first work is this. The twelve Sutras are divided into 2 Chapters of 6 Sutras each, general and special. These chapters are divided into two 'Iyals' each. Making a total division of the book into four, of three Sutras each. I have, however, divided the work into four chapters, indicating at the same time whether each belongs to the general or the special division.

The first chapter treats of the proof of the three entities or Padarthas, the second dealing with their further attributes or relationship, the third dealing with Sadana or modes of attaining the benefit of the knowledge of the three Padarthas, and the last dealing with the True End sought after by all mankind. The reader of Vyasa's Sariraka Sutra or Vedanta Sutra will observe that the divisions adopted in the latter work are the same as in Sivagnana Botham. Further each Sutra is divided into separate theses or arguments and Meikanda Deva has added his commentary called Varthika to each of these theses or arguments or Adhikarana as it is called. This Varthika commentary is in very terse prose and is the most difficult portion of the work. Meikanda Deva has added Udarana or analogies in verses of Venba Metre to each of the Adhikaranas. These Udarana are not similes of rhetoric but are logical analogies used as a method of proof. The reader's attention is particularly drawn to these analogies and he is requested to test these analogies with any rule of Western logic, and at the same time test the analogies ordinarily set forth in works on Hindu Philosophy published in English. **Sivagnana Siddhi** is divided into two books, **Parapaksham** and **Supaksham**. In the Parapaksham, all the Hindu systems from Charvaka Philosophy to Mayavadam are stated and criticised and it is similar to Sayana's Sarva Darsana Sangraha, and yet a cursory comparison will show the superior treatment of the former. The subject which Sayana or as he is better known in Southern

Sivagnana Botham of Meykanda Deva

India, Vidyaranyar has compressed in one chapter in a few pages, under the heading of Saiva Darsan, is treated by Arulnanthi Sivachariar in his Supaksham in 300 and odd stanzas, and the printed works with commentaries comprise about 2,000 and odd pages. The ground plan of this work is the same as that of Sivagnana Botham but it contains in addition a chapter on '**Alavei**' or Logic, an abstract of which has been also translated by Rev. H. R. Hoisington and published in the American Oriental Journal, Vol, iv. Though this is based on Sanskrit works on logic, yet an advance is made in a new classification of logical methods, predicates, &c. And this I might say of the genius of Tamil writers generally, though they have borrowed largely from Sanskrit, the subject receives altogether an independent and original treatment. As my old teacher used to observe, no doubt Gold from Sanskrit source is taken but before it becomes current coin, it receives the stamp or impress of the Tamil writer's genius.

Then about the date of these works, there is no data available to fix the exact time of these works. But that they must have been very old in manifest from the fact that they have supplied the form and even the language for nearly all the Tamil writers on philosophy and religion, excepting in **Thevaram** and **Thiruvachakam** and other works included in the **Saiva Thirumurai**. And there are also clear data to show that these works were anterior to the establishment of any of the great Saiva Adhinams or Mutts in Southern India and the great Namasivaya Desikar, who founded the Thiruvaduthurai Adhinam about 600 years ago, claimed to be the fifth or sixth in succession from Meikanda Deva and the disciples of this Mutt and Saivas generally call themselves as belonging to Meikandan Santhathi. One other fact which fixes this much more approximately, I must mention. Umapathi Sivachariar who is fourth in succession from Meikanda Deva, gives the date of his work, Sankarpanirakaranam in the preface of the work itself as 1235 of Salivahana Era. This will make the work therefore 582 or 583 years old and giving a period of 25 or 30 years for each of the Acharyas, the date of Meikanda Deva will be about A. D. 1192 or 1212 or say about A. D. 1200. These facts therefore furnish us with a positive data that these works could not have been at least less than 650 years old. I have not been however able to investigate the matter with all the available sources of information, for want of time and opportunity and I must leave the subject here.

A few words about the commentators on these works are also necessary. There are two short commentaries published on Sivagnana Botham. One is by Pandi Perumal and it is a very clear and useful commentary for the beginner and nothing is known about the writer and about his life except his mere name; but from the way he describes himself, he must have lived very near the time of Meikanda Deva. The other commentator is a well-known person, Sivagnana Yogi or Muniver who died in the year Visuvavasu before last, 1785 A. D. The famous Adhinam at Thiruvaduthurai has produced very many great sages, poets and writers in its days but it produced none equal to Sivagnana Yogi. The Tamil writers do not think that any praise is too lavish when bestowed upon him; and I have heard pundits of even other faiths speak in awe and respect of his mighty genius. He was a great Poet, and Rhetorician, a keen Logician and Philosopher, and commentator and a great Sanskrit Scholar. He with his pupil composed Kanchipuram which in the opinion of many surpasses many of the Epics in the Tamil language, so far as the imagery of its description and its great originality and the difficulty of its style and diction are concerned. He is the author of several commentaries and works on Tamil Grammar

Sivagnana Botham of Meykanda Deva

and Rhetoric. He has translated into Tamil the Sanskrit **Tarka Sangraha** and his commentaries on Sivagnana Botham and Sivagnana Siddhi have been rarely equalled for the depth of perception and clearness of exposition and the vastness of erudition displayed by him. His short commentary on Sivagnana Botham is the one now published and his other commentary called the Dravida Bhashya has not been published yet. The original manuscripts are in the possession of His Holiness the Pandara Sannadhigal of Thiruvavaduthurai and very many attempts were made during the life time of His Holiness the late Pandara Sannadhigal to induce him to publish this work but without success. I have interviewed His Holiness the Present Pandara Sannadhigal, and he appeared to me to be very enlightened in his views and sentiment and I have every hope that His Holiness will have no objection to publish the work provided he sees that the people are really earnest about its publication. A few glimpses that have been obtained of the work here and there fully justify the great expectations entertained of it as a work of very rare merit. Sivagnana Yogi has fully followed in his dialectics the dictum laid down by the author of Sivaprakasam that everything old is not necessarily true and that everything new is not necessarily false. This view accounts generally for the greater freedom of thought displayed by Tamil Siddhantha Philosophers in the treatment of their subject without being tied down too narrowly by any Vedic Text, &c., than Sanskrit writers.

In these days of boasted toleration, and the proclamation of universal truths and universal religions from every little house top, it will be interesting to note what an ideal of toleration and universal religion the Siddhanta writers generally had. Says the author of Sivagnana Siddhi, "Religions and truths as professed in this world are various and differ from each other. If you ask, which is then the true religion and which is the universal truth, hear! That is an universal Religion and Truth, which without contradicting this faith or that faith reconciles their differences and comprises all and every faith and truth in its broad folds." The gist of this is contained in the phrase 'எல்லாமாய் அல்லவுமாய்' "all and not all or above all" which again is the **Lakshana** of **Adwaitham**, as I have elsewhere explained. In India, at the present day, certain phrases or forms of Idealism are put forward as expressing universal Truth and a large body of ignorant and credulous people are misled by it. Idealism is being exploded and discredited in Europe, and as M. Barth truly observes, Idealism when pushed to its logical conclusions leads one to Nihilism.

The **Siddhanta Sastras** are 14 in number. The first is **Sivagnana Botham** of Meikanda Deva; and two works of Arulnanthi Sivachariar I have already mentioned. Another of Meikanda Deva's pupils by name Manavasakam Kandanthar composed a treatise called 'Unmai Vilakkam' 'Light of truth' and this little work contains an explanation of many a profound truth in Hindu Philosophy. Two works, **Thiru Unthiar** (திருவுந்தியார்) and **Thiru Kalitrupadiar** (திருக்களிற்றுபடியார்) are ascribed to a Sage **Uyavantha Devar**, who is said to have come from the north; and eight works were composed by Umapathi Sivachariar, the principal of which **Sivaprakasam** has been also translated by Rev. H. R. Hoisington. The authors of these treatises together with **Maraignana Sambanthar** are regarded by Saivas as their **Santhana Acharyas**, expounders of their Philosophy and Fathers of the Church as distinguished from their **Samaya Acharyas**, Thirugnana Sambanthar, Vakisar, Sundarar, and Manikavachakar who were authors of devotional works, and maintained the supremacy of

Sivagnana Botham of Meykanda Deva

their Vedic faith and Religion against Buddhism and Jainism, and but for whom the modern Hindus would be reading the Thripitaka and Jataka tales instead of our Vedas and Upanishads and works founded on them, and would be one with the Atheistical Siamese or the highly idolatrous and superstitious Chinese. And here I might take the liberty of addressing a few words to my Hindu countrymen, at least to those whose mother tongue is Tamil and who are born in the Tamil country and are able to read the Tamil language. It is not everybody who has the desire to study Philosophy or can become a Philosopher. To these, I would recommend the devotional works of our Saints, whether Saiva or Vaishnava. Unlike the Hindus of other parts of this vast Peninsula, it is the peculiar pride of the Tamilian, that he possesses a Tamil Veda, which consist of his Thevaram, Thiruvachakam and Thiruvaimozhi, and this is not an empty boast. As Swami Vivekananda observes, Vedas are eternal, as truths are eternal, and truths are not confined to the Sanskrit language alone. The authors of the Tamil Veda are regarded as avatars and even if not so; they were at any rate Jivan Muktas or Gnanis. And as I have explained in my notes to the Eleventh Sutra, these Jivan Muktas are true Bhaktas and they are all Love. And the Tamil Veda is the outpouring of their great Love. My old Christian teacher used to observe that the Dravidian is essentially and naturally a devotional man; and is this not so, because they had early received and imbibed the Great outpourings of Love of our Divine Saints? To the student or enquirer who is more ambitious and wishes to fathom the mysteries of nature, I cannot do better than recommend these very books as a first course and the conviction will surely dawn upon his mind as he advances in his study of Philosophy and compares what is contained in the Tamil Veda with the bare bones of Philosophy that he has nothing better for his last course than what he had for his first course; and as the Divine Tiruvalluvar says, what is the use of all philosophy and knowledge if it does not lead one to the worship of his Maker in all truth and in all love? However, as a course of philosophical study, the Siddhanta works contain the most highly developed and logically systematized thinking of the Hindus. And if it is thought necessary, a study of the Vedas and Upanishads may follow. Without this preliminary course, a study of the latter will only end one in chaos and confusion. I address these remarks as a student to a student, as one enquirer to another and I claim no more weight to my words.

I give below a stanza which shows in what high estimation, Tamilians hold the present work and other works referred to above.

"வேதம் பசு; அதன்பால் மெய்யாகமம்; நால்வர்
ஓதும் தமிழ் அதனின் உள்ளுறுநெய்; - போதமிகு
நெய்யின் உறுசுவையாம் நீள்வெண்ணெய் மெய்கண்டான்.
செய்ததமிழ் நூலின் திறம்."

(The Veda is the cow; the Agama is its milk; the Tamil (Thevaram and Thiruvachakam) of the four Saints, is the ghee churned from it; the excellence of the well instructive Tamil (Sivagnana Botham) of Meikanda Deva of Thiruvennainallur is like the sweetness of such ghee.)

Sivagnana Botham of Meykanda Deva

LIST OF AGAMA OR TANTRA.

1. Kamika	15. Vira
2. Yogaja	16. *Rourava*
3. Chinthia	17. Maguta
4. Karana	18. Vimala
5. Achitha	19. Chandra Gnana
6. Theeptha	20. Mukavimba
7. Sukshuma	21. Purorjita
8. Sakaschira	22. Lalitham
9. Anjuman	23. Chittam
10. Supprabetha	24. Santhana
11. Vijia	25. Sarvoktha
12. Nischuvasa	26. Kirana
13. Swayambhuva	27. Betha
14. Agneya	28. Vathula

LIST OF SIDDHANTA WORKS IN TAMIL.

1. Sivagnana Botham	15. Sivaprakasam
2. Sivagnana Siddhi	16. Kodikavi
3. Irupairupakthu	17. Vinavenba
4. Thiruvunthiar	18. Nenjuviduthoothu
5. Thirukalitrupadiar	19. Sankarapanirakaranam
6. Unmainerivilakam	20. Potripakrodai
7. Unmaivilakkam	21. Thiruvarutpayan

Sivagnana Botham of Meykanda Deva

ॐ
॥ शिवज्ञानबोधं ॥

स्त्रीपुत्रपुंसकादित्वाज्जगतः कार्यदर्शनात् ।
अस्ति कर्ता स हृत्वैतत् सृजत्यस्मात् प्रभुर्हरः ॥ १ ॥

अन्वस्सन्व्याप्तितोऽनन्यः कर्ता कर्मानुसारतः ।
करोति संसृतिं पुंसां आज्ञया समवेतया ॥ २ ॥

नेतितो ममतोद्रेकादक्षोपरतिबोधतः ।
स्वापे निर्भोगतो बोधे बोद्धृत्वादस्त्यणुस्तनी ॥ ३ ॥

आत्मान्तःकरणादन्योऽप्यन्वितो मन्त्रिभूपवत् ।
अवस्थापंचकस्य: स्यान्मलरुद्रखड्विक्रय ॥ ४ ॥

विदन्त्यक्षाणि पुंसार्थान्न स्वयंसोऽपि शंभुना ।
तद्विकारि शिवक्षेत्र कान्तोऽयोवत्स तं नयेत् ॥ ५ ॥

अदृश्यं चेदसद्भावो दृश्यं चेज्जडिमा भवेत् ।
शंभोस्तद्व्यतिरेकेण ज्ञेयं रूपं विदुर्बुधाः ॥ ६ ॥

नाचिच्चित्सन्निधौ किन्तु न चित्तस्मे उभे मिथ: ।
प्रपंचशिवयोर्वेत्ता उअस्स आत्मा तयोः पृथक् ॥ ७ ॥

स्थित्वा सहेन्द्रियव्याधैः त्वां न वेत्सीति बोधितः ।
मुक्त्वैतान् गुरुणानन्यो धन्यः प्राप्नोति तत्पदम् ॥ ८ ॥

चिद्दृशात्मनिदृष्टेषं त्यक्त्वा वृत्तिमरीचिकाम् ।
लब्ध्वा शिवपदच्छायां ध्यायेत्पंचाक्षरीं सुधीः ॥ ९ ॥

शिवेनैक्यं गतसिद्धस्तदधीनः खवृत्तिकः ।
मलमायाद्यसंसृष्टो भवति स्वानुभूतिमान् ॥ १० ॥

दृशोर्दर्शयिताक्ष्णात्मा तस्य दर्शयिता शिवः ।
तस्मात्तस्मिन्परां भक्तिं कुर्याद्दाल्मोपकारके ॥ ११ ॥

मुक्त्यै प्राप्य सतस्तेषां भजेद्द्वेषं शिवालयं ।
एव विद्याच्छिवज्ञानबोधे शैवार्थनिर्णयं ॥ १२ ॥

Sivagnana Botham of Meykanda Deva

உ
சிவமயம்

சிவஞான போதம்

சூத்திரம்

அவன் அவள் அது எனும் அவை மூவினைமையின்
தோற்றிய திதியே ஒடுங்கி மலத்து உளதாம்
அந்தம் ஆதி என்மனார் புலவர். 1

அவையே தானேயாய் இருவினையின்
போக்கு வரவு புரிய ஆணையின்
நீக்கம் இன்றி நிற்கும் அன்றே. 2

உளது இலதென்றலின் எனதுட லென்றலின்
ஐம்புலன், ஒடுக்கம் அறிதலின், கண்படில்
உண்டிவினை யின்மையின், உணர்த்த உணர்தலின்
மாயா வியந்திர தனுவினுள் ஆன்மா. 3

அந்தக் கரணம் அவற்றின் ஒன்றன்று,
சந்தித்தது ஆன்மா சகசமலத் துணராது
அமைச்சுஅரசு ஏய்ப்பநின்று அஞ்சவத் தைத்தே. 4

விளம்பிய உள்ளத்து மெய்வாய் கண் மூக்கு
அளந்தளந்து அறியா ஆங்கவை போலத்
தாம் தம் உணர்வில் தமியருள்
காந்தங் கண்ட பசாசத்து அவையே. 5

உணருரு எனின் அசத்து, உணராது எனின்
இன்மையின், இருதிறன் அல்லது சிவசத்தாம்என
இரண்டு வகையின் இசைக்கும் மன்னுலகே. 6

யாவையும் சூனியம் சத்து எதிர் ஆகலின்
சத்தே அறியாது அசத்து இலது அறியாது
இருதிறன் அறிவளது இரண்டலா(த) ஆன்மா. 7

ஐம்புல வேடரின் அயர்ந்தனை வளர்ந்து எனத்
தம்முதல் குருவுமாய்த் தவத்தினில் உணர்த்த விட்டு
அன்னியம் இன்மையின் அரன்கழல் செலுமே. 8

Sivagnana Botham of Meykanda Deva

ஊனக்கண் பாசம் உணராப் பதியை
ஞானக் கண்ணினில் சிந்தை நாடி
உராத்துணைத்தேர்த்து எனப் பாசம் ஒருவத்
தண்ணீழலாம் பதி, விதி எண்ணும் அஞ்செழுத்தே.   9

அவனே தானே ஆகிய அந்நெறி(யின்)
ஏகனாகி இறைபணி நிற்க
மலமாயை தன்னொடு வல்வினை இன்றே.   10

காணும் கண்ணுக்குக் காட்டும் உளம்போல்
காண உள்ளத்தைக் கண்டு காட்டலின்
அயரா அன்பின் அரன்கழல் செலுமே.   11

செம்மலர் நோன்தாள் சேரல் ஒட்டா
அம்மலங் கழிஇ அன்பரொடு மரீஇ
மாலற நேயம் மலிந்தவர் வேடமும்
ஆலயம் தானும் அரனெனத் தொழுமே.   12

Sivagnana Botham of Meykanda Deva

SIVAGNANA BOTHAM

I. As the (seen) universe, spoken of as he, she and it, undergoes three changes (origin, development, and decay), this must be an entity created (by an efficient cause.) This entity owing to its conjunction with *Anava Mala* has to emanate from *Hara* to whom it returns during *Samharam*. Hence, the learned say that *Hara* is the first cause.

II. He is one with the souls (*Abetha*). He is different from them (*Betha*). He is one and different from them (*Bethabetha*). He stands in *Samavaya* union with His Gnana Sakti and causes the souls to undergo the processes of evolution (births) and return (*Samharam*) by including their good and bad acts (*Karma*).

III. It rejects every portion of the body as not being itself; It says my body; it is conscious of dreams; it exists in sleep without feeling pleasure or pain or movements; it knows from others; This is the soul which exists in the body formed as a machine from *Maya*.

IV. The soul is not one of the *Andakarana*. It is not conscious when it is in conjunction with *Anavamala*. It becomes conscious only when it meets the *Andakarana*, just as a king understands through his ministers. The relation of the soul to the five *Avastha* is also similar.

V. The senses while perceiving the object cannot perceive themselves or the soul; and they are perceived by soul. Similarly, the soul while perceiving cannot perceive itself (while thinking cannot think thought) and God. It is moved by the *Arul Sakti* of God, as the magnet moves the iron, while Himself remains immoveable or unchangeable.

VI. That which is perceived by the senses is *Asat* (changeable.) That which is not so perceived does not exist. God is neither the one nor the other, and hence called *Siva Sat* or *Chit Sat* by the wise; *Chit* or Siva when not understood by the human intelligence and *Sat* when perceived with divine wisdom.

VII. In the presence of Sat, everything else (cosmos-Asat) is *Sunyam* (is non-apparent) Hence Sat cannot perceive *Asat*. As *Asat* does not exist, it cannot perceive *Sat*. That which perceives both cannot be either of them. This is the Soul (called *Satasat*).

VIII. The Lord appearing as *Guru* to the Soul which had advanced in *Tapas* (Virtue and Knowledge) instructs him that he has wasted himself by living among the savages of the five senses; and on this, the soul, understanding its real nature leaves its former associates, and not being different from Him, becomes united to His Feet.

IX. The soul, on perceiving in itself with. The eye of Gnanam, the Lord who cannot be perceived by the human intellect or senses, and on giving up the world (Pasa) by knowing it to be false as a mirage, will find its rest in the Lord. Let the soul contemplate *Sri Panchatchara* according to Law.

Sivagnana Botham of Meykanda Deva

X. As the lord becomes one with the Soul in its human condition, so let the Soul become one with Him and perceive all its actions to be His. Then will it lose all its Mala, Maya, and *Karma*.

XI. As the soul enables the eye to see and itself sees, so Hara enables the soul to know and itself knows. And this *Adwaitha* knowledge and undying Love will unite it to His Feet.

XII. Let the *Jivatma*, after washing off its *Mala* which separates it from the strong Lotus feet of the Lord and mixing in the society of *Bhaktas (Jivan Muktas)* whose souls abound with Love, having lost dark ignorance, contemplate their Forms and the Forms in the temples as His Form.

Sivagnana Botham of Meykanda Deva

INVOCATION OF GANESHA

The Good will crown their heads with the two Feet of *Ganesha* who was begotten by the Great Teacher, who sat under the Sacred Mountain Banyan tree and removed the doubts of the Great *Nandi*.

NOTES

Ganesha is the representation of Brahm and is of the Form of the *Samashti Pranava*. If the letters '*a*,' '*u*' and '*m*' represent severally '*Brahma, Vishnu* and *Rudra*,' *Ganesha* represents 'Aum' or 'Om'; and He is by pre-eminence therefore the Deity of the Pranava; and His Temples are therefore True *Pranava alayas*, without which no place, however insignificant, it may be, is found to exist throughout the length and breadth of India. As *Pranava* is the chief *Mantra* of the Hindus, and as nothing can be done without uttering it, hence the universal practice of invoking *Pillaiyar* before beginning any rite or work or treatise. '*Pillayar Shuli*' which heads this page is of course the Pranava symbol. The two feet here described are His *Gnana Sakti* and *Kriya Sakti*. The God is given the Elephant head as that is the one figure in nature which is of the Form of *Pranava*. See the subject further discussed in the notes to fourth Sutra. The author of 'Dravida Bhashya' points out how this couplet in praise of Ganesha or Ganapathi comprises in itself the subject matter of the whole of the Twelve Sutras. The two couplets indicate the subject into two chapters, general and special, and the four divisions of the two lines indicate the sub-division of the subject into four 'Iyals' or 'sub-chapters' and the twelve words the couplet contains indicate the twelve sutras and it is then pointed out how the subject matter is itself compressed in these words.

Sivagnana Botham of Meykanda Deva

THE AUTHOR'S APOLOGY

Those who know their Lord from the knowledge of themselves (their true nature), will not revile me and my work, as I am their own slave. Those who do not know themselves cannot know their Lord, and of course cannot agree among themselves. Their abuse I hear not.

SIVAGNANA BOTHAM

CHAPTER I. PRAMANAVIYAL – PROOF

I

FIRST SUTRA

ON THE EXISTENCE OF GOD

Sutra: - As the (seen) universe, spoken of as he, she and it, undergoes three changes (origin, development, and decay), this must be an entity created (by an efficient cause.) This entity owing to its conjunction with *Anava Mala* has to emanate from *Hara* to whom it returns during *Samharam*. Hence, the learned say that *Hara* is the first cause.

Commentary

This Sutram establishes by an inference that this universe has *Hara* as its First cause and it consists of three principal arguments.

First Argument

Choornika: - The universe undergoes the three changes of original production, development, and decay.

Varthikam: - As an existing object has its origin and decay, it is shown that the cosmic entity which is spoken of as he, she, and it is subject to origin, development and decav.

Udarana: -The world, if it exists, is followed by destruction and reproduction. Having seen that particular species in nature have particular seasons of reproduction, development, and decay, will not the wise argue that the world also undergoes periodical changes?

Second Argument

Choornika: - These changes are caused by *Hara*.

Varthikam: - Objects not in existence (unreal) do not come into visible being; hence the seen universe must be an entity. As products of industry cannot be produced except by an artisan, so the world which appears as a product has a Creator or an Efficient Cause. And the cosmos can only be developed from the condition into which it had been dissolved previously in *Samharam*.

Udarana: - (a) The world which has been resolved into *Hara* must emanate from Him. The dissolution is required as rest for *Karma Mala*, and the reproduction for the removal of *Anava Mala*. All will admit that things will be reproduced from what they had been resolved

Sivagnana Botham of Meykanda Deva

into. If you say that the world resolved into *Vishnu* whose form is Mulaprakriti, then all the higher products of *Maya* above *Mulaprakriti* will not be dissolved. All the products of *Maya* become resolved along with *Vishnu* and *Brahma* into *Hara* who is the author of both.

(*b*) Just as a sprout appears when a seed is embedded in moist earth, so the world is created from Maya by the *Sakti* or Light of *Iswara*, whose creation is in accordance with the unchangeable laws of *Karma*; and Lo! The Power of Sakti!

Just as, when not sprouting, the seed is concealed in the earth, so *Maya* exists in God when not differentiated. And he gives each his form as he desires it, just as the worm in a wasp's nest gets the form it desires.

(*c*) Just as Time the producer of all changes, itself remains without change, so God who creates, develops, and destroys the world without any mechanical means and by his mere will, remains without change. He has in consequence no ties (*Pasa Bantham*) just like the mind having certain impressions, itself remains different (i.e., does not become changed into them) and like the man who has learnt the truth in the waking state will not be misled by the dreams he has had.

or

God is eternal and like Time is without change when with His mere will and without any mechanical means, He creates, develops and destroys the world. His creation is without any purpose to Himself as the dreamer finds no benefit in his dreams in his waking state.

Third Argument

Choornika: - The other two (*Vishnu* and *Brahma*) are also subject to these three changes.

Varthikam: - As the known cosmic entity has no power of action except through the unknown author of *Samharam*, this author, *Hara* is the only supreme God.

Udarana: -   *Hara* who is neither the one nor the other in the Universe of mind and matter, is the only Supreme being of the said Universe, as the Universe of mind also becomes dissolved in Him in the same way, after they (minds) had been created and developed. The said Universe of mind which like Him is eternal is subordinate to Him even in *Moksha*.

NOTES

GENERAL:

The argument proceeds from a *Prathiatcha* fact admitted by the *Lokayitha* or materialist. This fact, the seen universe which can be described under the terms He, (masculine gender), She (feminine gender) or It (neuter gender) or as *Thanu* (animal Bodies), *Karma* (internal and external organs) or senses, *Buvana* (worlds) and *Bhoga* (sensations) is then shown to be capable of change or evolution. Its present condition is itself the product of causation, evolved from its primordial nature; and its decay is its resolution into its primordial state. This

Sivagnana Botham of Meykanda Deva

primordial substance is what is called *Maya* or cosmic matter. This *Maya* is not a non-entity nor is it caused from God or *Atma* (soul) as will be shown later on. The definition of Maya and its treatment will include all the phenomena noted by the present-day Materialist and Biologist in the field of Physics and Biology. It is best translated by the word "object and object consciousness." This "Maya" therefore undergoes *Srishti, Sthithi* and *Samharam*; Samharam is not destruction and the chain of evolution does not stop but it proceeds; and the reason for this successive change *i. e.* recreation and rebirths is given in the text 'மலத்துளதாம்.' it is caused by or necessitated by its conjunction with *Anava Mala*. The word Anava is derived from the root "Anu" meaning exceedingly small and the word *Anu* which is a synonym for soul, is so called, as the soul which is a *Vibhu* in its real state is made *Anu* (small as an atom) by its conjunction with *Anava Mala*. This Anava Mala is the imperfection or ignorance or impurity or darkness which covers or conceals the intelligence or light or purity of the soul. It is the presence of this imperfection or impurity in nature, which necessitates Evolution or Successive Recreations and Rebirths, as it can only be removed by such evolution. Maya is therefore evolved but not by its own inherent power. Maya or Matter is capable of motion but cannot move itself; just as a wheel capable of motion cannot move unless moved by some other person or thing or by the force of gravity, or just as products of industry cannot shape themselves except through an artificer and his instruments or tools, though they possess such capability. This grand Force, then, which moves and evolves the whole universe is the First cause, and the grand Artificer, the Supreme Being. *Maya* is the material cause, *Upadana Karma* of the universe, supplying its form and matter; God is the efficient cause or *Nimitha Karana*; and the *Thunai Karana, Sahakari* or instrumental cause is His *Chit Sakti* which is defined in the second sutra.

The inference employed here is an inductive inference and the argument is represented by two syllogistic Forms called *Kevalanvayi Anumana* and *Anvaya Vyatireki Anumana*. The first syllogism is represented like this.

(1) *Pratidgna* - Proposition.

    This universe has a Karta.

(2) *Hetu* - The reason.

    Because it has been evolved into forms such as he, she and it.

(3) *Utharana* - The instance.

    A pot is made by a potter.

(4) *Upanayam* - The assumption.

    The universe is such a product as a pot.

(5) *Nigamana* - The deduction.

    Therefore, the universe has a Karta.

Sivagnana Botham of Meykanda Deva

For further forms see the commentaries of Sivagra Yogi on *Sivagnana Siddhi*.

The word *Samhara* which means change connotes both Srishti and Sthithi and hence Hara who is Samhara Karta represents in Himself the Powers of Srishti and Sthithi Kartas. In fact when we look at the universe and postulate God, the one idea we have of Him is as The Supreme Evolving Energy or Force working for the perfection of Salvation of the world of Mind and Matter. The root meaning of Hara is change producer or destroyer. He evolves the world and removes darkness or *Agnana*.

An *adhikarana* or argument comprises (1) *Vishaya* - The proposition (2) *Samsaya* - The doubt or objections (3) *Purvapaksha* - The Theory refuted, (4) *Siddhanta* - The Theory proved or established and (5) *Sankathi* - The sequence in the argument.

And it is a point worthy of note how in the treatment of the whole subject, the argument proceeds step by step one based upon or following the first without a single break in the chain. And it is also possible to exhibit each argument in the five modes abovementioned; but it is unnecessary to do so.

Choornika is a particular style of expression. It expresses in a short sentence the substance of the whole argument.

Varthikam means an explanatory note.

Udarana or analogy is here used as a method of inductive proof and should be distinguished from the various kinds of *Upamana* Polis or false analogies and figures of rhetoric. The sole condition of a real analogy is, as stated by Dr. Bain, that the sameness apply to the attribute found by induction to bear the consequence assigned.

1.   The first argument needs no comment; no body now denies that Cosmos undergoes successive evolutionary changes.

2.   The second argument in fact consists of three arguments. The first argument refutes the theory of Buddhists and Mayavathis (Idealists) who assert the non-reality of the universe. The 2nd argument refutes the theory that world can evolve of itself; and the third deals with the mode of evolution i.e., by dissolution and reproduction.

(*a*)   The first illustration shows the reason why dissolution is required. It is as rest for *Karma*; just after the exertions of the day, we require rest during the night for undergoing the struggles of tomorrow, so death gives us a prolonged rest to the human monad to enable it to eat its previous Karma in the next birth. Why should it have a next birth? Because it must eat the fruits of previous *Karma* and unless it does so, its *Anava Mala* or Ignorance cannot be removed. This latter then is the reason for reproduction.

(*b*)   The seed is the Maya; the sprout, the Karma; and the tree, the world; and the Earth, God; and its moisture and heat, the Sakti of God. God is "*Viyapaka*." Souls are *Vyapti* and Maya and other Mala are *Vyappia*. Sea is *Vyapaka*, water is the *Vyapti* and the salt is *Vyappia*.

Sivagnana Botham of Meykanda Deva

The text of the Veda.

"That the worlds are created out 'of Brahm'", is to be understood as when we say that the tree sprung out of the earth; of, also the word Pangaja meaning sprung out of mire.

It is *Karma* that determines the number of successive births and creations and the forms in succession, and not God. Though it is the worm which passes into various forms before it becomes the wasp, yet without the aid of the parent wasp which affords it warmth and food, the worm cannot obtain its full development, so God adjusts the birth according to Karma and makes the souls eat the fruits thereof. Without His Divine Presence and Energy the soul cannot take for itself its own material body and it can have no progress unless when it is in conjunction with its material body. It is in Him we live, move, and have our very being.

(c) The question arises whether God in producing these changes does change in any way. When one man reaps good and another reaps evil, does God like the one and dislike the other?

This is answered in the negative, in the illustration. He is Nirvikari. He has neither likes nor dislikes. (வேண்டுதல் வேண்டாமையிலான் - Kural).

One other illustration given in the 2nd Sutra and elaborated by the commentator of *Ozhivilodukham* is as follows: "The sun shines without any desire or intention or volition on its part, yet in its presence, the lotus plant receives its development and while one flower is still a bud, another has fully blown out and a third is withering; So, in the Divine Presence, Maya undergoes changes and so the author says "சந்நிதிக்கே அஞ்சு தொழிலாம்." (His Presence possesses five functions).

One other peculiarity in the nomenclature of God employed by the various schools and affecting the various ideals formed, deserves to be noted here. The Vaishnava would hardly describe God in any other form than masculine. All specific names of Vishnu are masculine and they cannot be declined in any other gender and even when so declined they will not denote Vishnu, e. g. Vishnu, Vaishnavi, and Vaishnavam and Narayana, Narayani, and Narayanam. And of course, the image which the use of the word calls up is a male form. A follower of Sankaracharya would prefer to use a neuter form of expression and calls his God, *Brahm*, *Param* and so on, though with his peculiar adaptability he would also use such words as Narayana, *Iswara*, *Isa*, &c. the Saiva however uses all the three forms. 'He, She and It' in describing God, and all the specific names of *Siva* are capable of declension in all the three forms without change in its denotation and connotation. Siva, Sivah, Sivam; Iswara, Iswari, Iswaram; Sankara, Sankari, Sankaram; Para, Parah, Param and so on. And accordingly the images which he employs in his temples correspond to these forms. All nature is comprised in the three forms he, she and it. And when we use human language and forms of Nature to describe Him, there is no reason why one form should be preferred to the other, when all forms of Nature are His.

I may note here another peculiar doctrine of this School.

Sivagnana Botham of Meykanda Deva

In fact if there is any one doctrine which is more insisted on in this School than any other, it is this that God cannot be born in the flesh and He cannot have human Avatars. It is the height of absurdity to suppose that God who is the inconceivable and the unknowable and indescribable (வாக்குமனாதீதம்) can be born as a man when He ceases to be such. (See notes to sixth Sutra for a further discussion of the point).

(3) This argument establishes the supremacy of Hara and the One-ness of God.

The commentaries here discuss why God is not Brahma or Vishnu or Atma or the rest, the answer being that these latter are all liable to change and possess no *Swathanthram*; and why there should not be too many Gods as *Aneka Iswara Vathis* assert and several other questions besides.

It should here be noted that Hara or Siva or Isa or Iswara as used in the text is not to be identified with one of the Hindu Trinity bearing the same name. In the whole of the sacred literature we find Him described as the Lord of the Trinity, and as One who cannot be known even to the Trinity. The Trimurthis are themselves regarded as Mortals, being born at the beginning of each Kalpa and dying at the end of each. And the Vishnu of the text means only the Puranic Vishnu, clothed with such attributes and personal qualities as are ascribed to Him and capable of Avatars and the Vishnu of the Trinity representing Mula Prakriti and the function of Sthithi.

Concluding remarks

The first Sutra therefore establishes the existence of the three Mala, (Maya, Anava, and Karma) and of God. In the terminology of this School, the three Mala are called by a generic name Pasa and God is called Pathi. Pasa means, a bond or tie or shackle, or Bantham, and the three Banthams are distinguished as follows: -

Anava Pasa binds or limits the Omniscience or Perfect Knowledge of the Soul and hence called Prathibantham.

Karma Pasa like an unceasing flood follows the Soul and drives it to eat the fruits of karma (Bhoga) without permitting it to seek Moksha and hence called Anubandham.

Maya Pasa limits the Omnipresence (Vyabaka) of the Soul and confines it to a Particular body and hence called Sambantham.

Atma in the terminology of this School is called Pasu as a thing bound by Pasa. The terminology employed by the Ramanujas for these Thripadarthas is chit, achit and Iswara and that by the school of Sankaracharya is Jagat, Jiva, and Para.

The next Sutra proceeds to define Chit Sakti by which alone the relation between God and Atma and Mala is established and by whose Power alone Re-births are induced.

Sivagnana Botham of Meykanda Deva

II
SECOND SUTRA

THE RELATION OF GOD TO THE WORLD AND TO SOULS

Sutra: - He is one with the souls (*Abetha*). He is different from them (*Betha*). He is one and different from them (*Bethabetha*). He stands in *Samavaya* union with His Gnana Sakti and causes the souls to undergo the processes of evolution (births) and return (*Samharam*) by including their good and bad acts (*Karma*).

Commentary
This treats of the subject of Rebirths and consists of 4 principal arguments.

First Argument
Choornika: - Hara exists in all the souls inseparably (as one with them.)

Varthikam: - The word Adwaitham cannot mean oneness or *Ekam*; as without a second, no one can think of himself as one, and as the very thought implies two things. The word simply denies the separate existence and separability of the two. In this sense, it is said here that the souls exist as one with the Lord.

Udarana: - (*a*) The soul, standing in its body composed of bones, muscles, &c., and in union with the senses, answers to the name given for its body, when anybody addresses it, and identifies itself with the body. Similarly, though the Lord stands in a similar intimate relation with the soul, He is not the soul, and the soul cannot become the Lord. In the human state, He is one and not one with the soul.

(*b*) The vedic Text, '*Ekam evadwithiyam Brahma*' '*Ekam Eva Rudra Nadwitiyaya thas theh*' means that there is only one Supreme Being without a second. And this one is the Pathi and not the soul. You who say (ignorantly) you are one (with the Lord) are the soul and are bound up with *Pasa*. As we say that without (the primary sound) 'A' all other letters will not sound, so the Vedas say "without the Lord, no other things will exist."

(*c*). The *Arul Sakti* of the Lord which pervades the whole universe is inseparably and eternally connected with the world, just like the sound in the tune and the flavor in the fruit. So, the rare Vedas declare that *Brahm* is *Adwaitham* and not *Ekam* with the universe.

(*d*) Just like the whetstone composed of gold, wax and sand, God is one with the world and is different from it and He is neither (Bethabetham). When God enters my soul, when I am freed from Pasam, I identify myself with God, and say I am all the world.

Sivagnana Botham of Meykanda Deva

Second Argument

Choornika: - *Hara* makes the souls eat the fruit of their Karma.

Varthikam: - The soul's good and bad *Karma* are induced by the Gnana Sakti of the *Lord*; just as a king protects his town by appointing watchmen to guard it and thus exercises his authority.

Udarana: - (*a*) The soul joining the body caused by its previous *Karma* eats the fruits thereof. Similarly, our present actions (*Karma*) furnish the seed for our body in the next birth. God the all bountiful makes the soul eat the fruits of previous *Karma* (without suffering any change) just as the soil makes the cultivator reap as he sowed.

(*b*) Just as iron is attracted to the magnet when a person brings it in position, so the souls performing *Karma* join the body in which the *Karma* is effected and eat the fruits by the *Arul* of God. If they do not so enjoy by His Arul, who else could know and make them eat the fruits of Karma in the most unchangeable manner, in that condition, where they lie helpless, without self-knowledge, and self-action, enshrouded by *Mala*.

(*c*) The husk of the paddy or the rust of the copper is not new but co-existed with the grain or copper; so, the three *Malas, Maya, Karma* and *Anava* co-exist with the soul and were not acquired by it at any intermediate time. These undergo change in the presence of God, just as the Sun's rays cause one Lotus to open and another to close.

Third Argument

Choornika. - The souls are subject to re-births losing their previous forms.

Varthikam. - The souls are re-born after death as birth and death are possible only to things existing eternally and changing continually.

Udarana: - (*a*) The soul passing at death from its *Sthula Sarira* composed of eyes, ears, &c., into its *Sukshuma Sarira* which it had already, undergoes its experiences in Heaven or Hell; and forgetting such experiences, just as a dreamer forgets his experience of the waking state, passes as an atom in its *Sukshuma* state into a suitable womb at conception time, impelled thereto by the desire created by its previous *Karma*.

(*b*) The analogies of the serpent passing out of its old skin and the mind from the conscious into the dream condition and the *Yogi* into another body are often properly pointed out to explain the passing of the soul from its *Sthula* into the *Sukshuma Sarira*. Against this view, the analogy of the air of the pot passing into the atmosphere after the breaking of the pot, is instanced to support the view, that the soul takes no other body after death. This does not serve; it only illustrates the fact of the soul passing from the *Sukshuma Sarira* itself.

Sivagnana Botham of Meykanda Deva

Fourth Argument

Choornika: - *Hara* is omnipresent.

Varthikam: - He is one with His *chit-sakti*, as He is omnipresent without being one or different from the world.

Udarana: - If God is all-pervading (one with the souls and matter), He cannot be one. If he is two, He cannot be all-pervading. (He cannot be said to be not all-pervading as) there is no body or soul which exists without Him. He pervades everything by His *chit-sakti*, just like the light of the Sun. the whole universe is His property and the souls are His servants.

NOTES

GENERAL

This Sutra discusses the most important and peculiar doctrine of this school, namely its theory of Adwaitham or the relation between God and the souls. Three Relations are possible.

(1) Succession or causation. When one thing is the cause and the other is the effect, there is no difference whatever. It is *Abetha*; just like gold and ornaments made out of it (பொன்பணிபோல் அபேதம்).

(2) Co-existence with mutual exclusion. Here one has no connection whatever with the other. One is totally external to the other. It is *Betha* like darkness and light (இருள் ஒளிபோல் பேதம்).

(3) Co-existence without mutual exclusion or externality as when two different things are connected inseparably like the association of ideas. It is *Bethabetham*; just like the word and its meaning. Here the word is either a sound or a symbol and is distinguishable from the connotation of the name yet both the symbol or sound and the connotation is inseparably and indissolubly associated with each other. This relationship is not postulated by any other school. Under the first division comes in both Idealism (Mayavatham) and Materialism (Nasthikam and Boudha Vadham). In both the schools, causation is postulated whether it be that matter is derived from mind or the universe of mind and matter is derived from an Absolute or mind is derived from matter or a combination of Skandas. From the theory of causation, when you derive matter from mind, it will be as easy to derive mind from matter. And the objections we can take against the Materialist will equally be applicable to the theory of the Idealist, as is pointed out by Prof. G. J. Romanes in his article on Mind and Body. In fact, Idealism is regarded by the Siddhanti as Nastikam or Nihilism and the term Prachanna Bouddha Vadham is freely applied to it. The Hindu Idealists are also fond of giving two other analogies. The Spider and its web and the fire and its spark. It is easily seen that these are identical in substance and the web is merely the product of the material body, the glands of the Spider and not of its life Principle. The Siddhanthins therefore reject these relationships or at least the relationship pointed to by these analogies. The Visishtadwaita of Ramanujacharya and the Dwaitha of Madhwacharya may be placed under the second head or even the third head as some sort of

Sivagnana Botham of Meykanda Deva

relationship is said to exist between God and Man. In the Moksha of a Ramanuja, each atma retains its personality distinct from God but there is a union between its spirit and the universal spirit and according to the Mathwa the relationship is similar to that of a Guru and Sishya or that of a parent and child.

I said before that the Siddhantin rejects all these relationships in this sense that he does not affirm causation nor separable or inseparable co-existence as explained above. Yet in the Sutra God is called Abetha; the connection is such that an identity is perceived and the best illustration of this relationship is that of the body and life or mind (உடல் உயிர்போல் அபேதம்). The objective and subjective phenomena are quite different and yet a sort of absolute identity is established. He is Betha and this is illustrated as follows: -

An act of Perception is one and indivisible. Yet the perception is caused by two agencies the Eye and the Sun or Light. The Eye cannot perceive without the aid of the light, and though both the light of the Eye and the light of the Sun combine together, the combination is perceived as one. Here there is no causation as between the Eye and the Sun (கண் அருக்கன் போல் பேதம்). He is *Bethabetham*; but the Tamil equivalent of the latter word உடன் or உடனுமாய் is perhaps more expressive. This relationship is similar to that of the soul or mind and the sense of sight or eye (கண்ணெணாளியின் ஆன்மபோதம்போல் பேதாபேதம்). Though in all these cases an identity is perceived a difference in substance is also felt. It is this relation which could not easily be postulated in words, but which may perhaps be conceived and which is seen as two (Dwaitham) and at the same time as not two (Na Dwaitham); It is this relation which is called Adwaitham (a unity or identity in duality) and the Philosophy which postulates it, the Adwaitha Philosophy. And the 1st argument deals with the meaning and force of this word.

1. God is all (Prapancham) but all is not God. He is therefore all and not all. He is immanent in everything and yet above everything. This doctrine is very popular in nearly the whole of the Tamil Literature, and it is most vividly expressed in the favourite phrase (எல்லாமாய் அல்லவுமாய்). The Hindu Idealists stop with "எல்லாமாய்" "He is all" and do not proceed to postulate "அல்லவுமாய்." "He is not all" or "He is above all." All objective phenomena may be in a sense mental or subjective but all the subjective phenomena are not objective.

Adwaitham does not mean ஏகம் or Monism. The negative prefix '*a*' or '*na*' does not negative the positive existence of one or other of the two (Dwaitham). It is not used in the "*Abhava*" or இன்மைப்பொருள். If it is so used, it will not only negative one thing or other but it may negative both, and end in Nihilism; and it may not only mean one "Ekam or Monism" but may mean more than two i.e., three or any number. As the learned Commentator Sivagnana Yogi points out, when the negative is prefixed to the numeral, in common usage, it does not mean இன்மை or அபாவம். For instance, when we say "There are not two books in the room" "அறையில் இரண்டு புஸ்தகமில்லை" it may mean that "no books are in the room" or that "only one book is in the room" or that "there are more than two books."

Sivagnana Botham of Meykanda Deva

If the negative prefix in Adwaitham does not mean "Abhava" what does it mean? It is used in the "அன்மைப்பொருள்" or அல்ல 'non-dual sense.' The querist sees or fancies he sees two objects and asks 'are they dual'? The answer is 'They are non-dual' - இரண்டு அல்ல not meaning one. Adwaitham therefore means literally Non-dualism and not Monism. Cf. The word 'Anekam' which does not mean obviously ஒன்றில்லை (nothing) but 'ஒன்றல்ல' 'பல' (many). In Sivagnana Siddhi, Adwaitham is defined as ஒன்றாகாமல், இரண்டாகாமல், ஒன்று மிரண்டு மின்றாகாமல் (neither one, nor two, nor neither). The position seems to be a negative than a positive one. All this language is adopted so as to illustrate that the relation is such that it is not possible to adequately to examine or illustrate and we find the author of Ozhivilodukkam enjoin "ஏக மிரண்டென்னாமற் சும்மாயிரு." (Don't say one or two). Another popular verse runs as follows. "சும்மாயிரு சொல்லறவென்றலுமே அம்மாபொருளொன்று மறிந்திலனே." The subject is more fully treated in the subsequent chapters. If there is only one Absolute, the very idea of duality is impossible. The word Adwaitham implies the existence of two things and does not negative the reality or existence of one of the two. It simply postulates a relation between the two.

(a) This contains the illustration of body and mind. As in a purely objective state no subjective feeling is present, so in the human state, the soul is in a purely objective condition, and is not cognisant therefore of its subject God. The Atma is capable of a double relation; it has two kinds of Adwaitham. It is in Adwaitha relation with Maya and at the same time in Adwaitha relation with God. I may call the first its objective relation and the other its subjective relation. When its objective relation (its connection with Thanu, Karana, &c.) predominates, it is in Banda, it is the embodied human soul. When its subjectivity predominates, it is itself, it is in God, and it is God (*Moksha*). In its first condition, we don't see the soul but its object side, physical body and organs, mind, (manas) chittam, &c., and sensations and the worlds. In its second condition, we don't see the soul either but God with which it had identified itself. The important point to be noted is that though in the one or the other condition of the soul, one thing (God) or other (Maya) is not present, yet its existence or reality cannot be denied. In as much as we cannot see God now, we cannot deny His existence and call him *Mitya* (illusion) and when the world therefore disappears in the other case, nor can the world be called *Mitya*. Cf.

THAYUMANAVAR

"ஆணவத்தோ டத்துவிதமானபடி மெஞ்ஞானத்
தாணுவினோ டத்துவிதமாகுள் எந்நாளோ."

'O for the day, when I will become one with the Being of True knowledge as I am now one with Anava."

The subject receives further elaboration as we proceed.

(b) The illustration herein contained is the same as in the first verse of the sacred Kural, though its significance is not often understood. The point of comparison is not the position of the letter 'A' in place. Its place is to be sought in its origin and its power of determining other

Sivagnana Botham of Meykanda Deva

sounds as herein indicated. The most primary sound that the human organ can utter is 'a' and the other vowels (that can be sounded of themselves) are formed by modifications of 'a'; consonants on the other hand do not have the same origin as 'a' but they cannot be pronounced except with the help of 'a' and its modifications. So, though God and Man are distinct eternal entities, one(man) cannot exist except in God, but man does not originate from God as consonants do not originate from vowels. The same applies with regard to soul and its body (உயிர், மெய்) and it is this philosophic thought that underlies the Tamil equivalents of vowel and consonant (உயிர்மெய்).

The embodied soul or mind is the உயிர்மெய்.

(அ 'a') is the soul (K' 'க்') is the human body. In (க) embodied soul we see only the (body) consonant and not the vowel (soul). (அ 'a') again is God; 'க்' 'K' is the soul; In 'க' 'K' Human Soul, we see only the consonant (soul) and not the vowel (God though) you will realise both when you pronounce it (attain Gnanam).

God is the Life (உயிர்) and the Soul is His body and not a particle of The Life, (God) nor a spark from it, nor its reflection nor shadow nor the imagined silver in the oyster shell. In the latter case the soul is either a nonentity or there is no difference in kind or substance though there may be a difference in quantity or quality. In the former case, there is a difference in substance but an identity in fact as the two exist together.

(c) *Sakti* literally means power. And the *Sakti* of the Lord is therefore His Energy or Power, His Will and His Light or Grace or Knowledge. Hence, we have Three forms of *Sakti*, *Kriya Sakti*, *Itcha Sakti*, and *Gnana Sakti*, or *Arul Sakti*. God by his first two Powers evolves the universe from their undifferentiated condition. By the last He links the whole world to Himself. It is the Arul Sakti which connects God and Man. It is this Gnana Sakti which gives life to inanimate beings, harmony to things without harmony and to each and everything its peculiar beauty or taste or brightness. Without *It* everything else would be void, lifeless, actionless and darksome. This life of life, This Light of Light, This Chit Sakti is not the Light which Mr. Subba Row says enters some mechanism and becomes converted into a Human monad, man, and then becomes clothed with all the laws of Karma, &c., (Notes to Bag pp. 16 and 17). If so, what is it worth? Nor is Mr. Subba Row's Ishwara which he derives in a mysterious way from Brahm, the Ishwara of the Siddanthi. His Ishwara is Brahm and the Sakti is the Maha Sakti or Mahachaitanyam. The relation of Ishwara to Sakti to all other life is well illustrated in the Puranic story of Kumara Sambhava. God separated from his Sakti. He was then in a condition of a Yogi. Then all life did not become extinct but all life became lifeless, from the immortal Gods to the lowest things in the order of creation. The immortals became aware of this and of its cause and then planned a scheme to bring together Siva (sat) and Sakti (chit) as though they could do it. The very attempt proved a disastrous failure. They ignorantly thought, judging from their own stand-point that the God's Love was something akin to man's gross love. They therefore induced Manmatha or Kama Deva, the Human God of Love to aim his shafts at Siva. He did so and he was burned to ashes the very instant from a spark from His Nether Eye. He was however moved to pity at the sad plight of the so-called Immortals, became

Sivagnana Botham of Meykanda Deva

united to His Sakti, i.e., became all Love and begot Kumara who represents again Action or Energy and Gnana (His two Saktis) and who trampled under His foot Surapadma (All Evil) and released the Immortals from their bondage. This first Light (Adi Sakti) is Gayatri. (See the elaboration of this subject in Devi Bagavata Purana).

(*d*) (1) This contains another illustration. The whetstone is God in union with the world. The Gold wax is God, which holds and binds in itself the sands which are souls.

(2) The second portion of this stanza illustrates the principles of Sohambavana which underlies every Mantra from Pranava downwards. The devotee (Jivatma) is made to contemplate ("I am the Atma, God"), and he becomes one with God (Adwaitha). This is the process of identification. The author points out when he can be able to say "I am all the world." This is also the principle which underlies the teaching of Bagavat Gita, Krishna is the Jivan Mukta who by his holiness has identified himself with God, Iswara. He as Guru imparts teaching to his pupil Arjuna; and Sivagnana Yogi observes, "Is it not by this process of Sohambavana that Krishna when teaching Gita to Arjuna says 'I am all the world' and shows the Lord's Vivaswarupa in himself and teaches him to worship him and him alone leaving all other Gods; and Arjuna who believed in him firmly and understood the true significance of his word, performed Siva Pujah till his life's end, and the flowers showered by him on Krishna in Divine worship appeared on the sacred person of the Lord. Krishna as one who received Siva Diksha (initiation) from Upamanya Maharishi and had perfected himself in the knowledge of himself and his Lord, had perfected himself in Sohambavana."

The author anticipates here in fact what is elaborated in the third chapter, on "Sadana."

2. The good and bad Karma are what the soul had acquired during its previous birth which now lie at rest bound up with the resolved Maya. To quicken them into being again, the Chit Sakti of the Lord as the instrumental cause (துணைக்காரணம்) operates. This Sakti is likened to the authority of a King, hence called Agnja Sakti. It is in fact the source of all Authority and of all Law. A king exercises his authority by moving his limbs of the law, his officers; such a limb of the Supreme Law is the law of Karma. A king covers himself under the shield of his law from any imputations of partiality, &c., when he metes out reward or punishment. So also, God is not open to this charge. The universal Law determines the Law of Karma and the latter determines what each should undergo, either pleasure or pain, the working of this law is shown in the illustrations.

(*a*) The simple statement of this law of Karma is that he reaps as he sows and follows the laws of causation and conservation most rigidly. As no effect, can be produced without a cause, a man's body in his present life and his actions could not have been got adventitiously. Of course, God would not have given it of His mere will, as opposed to His Law as otherwise he would be open to the charge of partiality and lacking in Swathanthram. A being which is at the command of caprice has no control of itself. This therefore brings out the phrase 'உள்ளதே தோற்று' in the original, (What existed before appears now) and which I have simply translated as 'Previous Karma'. The seed which one gathers in the previous existence developes and matures in the soil (Lord's Power) becomes a tree (body) and bears good or bad fruits (pleasure or pain. Punyam or Papam). Without the soil the seed will not bear fruit; so without God, the past Karma will not bear fruit.

I may note here a definition of *Punyam* and *Papam* given by the late Sankara Pandithar of Jaffna. "Punyam" is "உயிர்க்கிதம் செய்தல்" - acts tending to give pleasure to sentient beings 'Papam' is 'உயிர்க்கதம் செய்தல்' acts tending to give pain to sentient beings.

The fruits of previous Karma eaten in this life form *Praraptha Karma*. In the process of eating, other acts are performed which form the seed for a future crop. And these acts form *Akamia Karma*; the seeds gathered for a future crop when sown become *Sanchitha Karma*. What is *Akamia* in this life is *Sanchitha* for the next.

(*b*) The last proposition in the last stanza is that the actions themselves will not bear fruits and make the soul eat them. The question is now asked why should not the soul choose its own actions and reap the fruits. This is answered in this illustration. It has not got the power of taking its body, whereby the Karma has to be performed. This has to be done by God. The cultivator (soul) cannot himself produce the tree (body) however he might try. He requires for this the medium of the soil (God). This inability is caused by the soul's want of self-knowledge and self-action, being covered by Anava Mala. In plainer language, no man would do a particular act tending to produce evil if he had the full knowledge to calculate all its consequences. It is therefore man's ignorance that is the cause of all evil. The only assumption here is that man in his original state is ignorant or imperfect or is shrouded by Agnanam or Anava. Grant this; and start the soul in the cycles of evolution, then the whole law of Karma comes into operation. This doctrine therefore is not to be confounded with the doctrine of Fate or necessity. Evolution or births are the only modes provided for attaining perfect knowledge; and for getting births or setting us on the wheel of Evolution we require God's help. This original assumption is treated of in the next illustration.

(c) That man is ignorant in knowledge (சிற்றறிவு) and is imprudent in his actions (சிறு தொழில்) is a fact and is taken as a fact by this school and is not converted into a Myth or Athyasam by a process of verbal jugglery. The explanation offered by the Idealists is no explanation at all, as after all the explanations offered, the final fact to be accounted for, still remains unexplained, namely Ignorance or Agnanam or Aviddhei, the cause of all evil, of all pain. We can explain a joint effect by assigning the laws of the separate causes; or we may explain an antecedent and consequent by discovering the intermediate links; or the explanation may consist in reducing several laws into one more general Law. None of these modes are adopted by the latter school but the explanation attempted falls clearly within one or other modes of fallacious or illusory explanations; and as Dr. Bain points out, the greatest fallacy of all is the supposition that something is to be desired beyond the most generalized conjunction or sequences of phenomena; and instancing the case of the union of body and mind, he observes that the case does not admit of any other explanation except that body and mind are found in union. When we arrive at a final fact, it is absurd to attempt a further explanation. What I have therefore treated of as an assumption in the concluding sentence of the last Para is no assumption at all, but a final fact of our nature. Our nature as it is, is imperfect, or adopting the

Sivagnana Botham of Meykanda Deva

language of the text, is enshrouded in impurity, Mala, Anava Mala. Law of universal Progression or Progress is another law of Nature; and Evolution or births we require an Omniscient and Perfect, *Ninmala Being*. In the whole chain of argument, this last is the only thing assumed or inferred. But see the argument on the other side. There is one Brahm. Ishwara is generated from the Brahm. Mulaprakriti is produced between them. Light or Energy proceeds from Ishwara and a particle of this Light becomes evolved into a man, or an ass, or a worm. All these are assumptions pure and simple. Mere hypothesis, it is admitted. Does this Hypothesis stand to reason? Does it furnish us any satisfactory reasons for all this evolution from Brahm to man or brute. Mr. Subba Row after stating that the First cause which is *Omnipresent* (what this really means is explained in the next argument) and *eternal* - is subject to periods of activity (Srishti) and passivity (Samharam) observes "But even the real reason for this activity and passivity is unintelligible to our minds" or as a learned Swami more *explicitly* and *honestly* puts it "Why should the Free, Perfect and pure Being be thus under the thralldom of matter? How can the Perfect soul be deluded into the belief that he is imperfect? How can the Perfect become the quasi perfect; How can the Pure, the Absolute change even a microscopically small part of its nature? The answer is 'I do not know.'"

You assume that evil or impurity is produced out of good or Purity and then parade your honesty and admit that you don't know why it is so. Don't you think that the fallacy lies more in your assumption than in any real difficulty? Why should you assume that evil is produced out of good? The thing is impossible; you must take things as they are. You find Good and Evil together. Man is impure and weak; it is just possible there is a Being who is pure and strong enough to lift him from the bottomless pit. And herein is the real reason "மலத்துளதாம்" as the Text says. God is active or passive as it is necessary for man to be set on the wheel of Evolution or to rest. Neither will it do to assume that God created Man at a particular moment and that he committed sin, and sin came into the world after the creations of Man and the world. Man, *committed sin*, because he had not the understanding to see that his good lay in obeying Gods words and he had not the free knowledge or intelligence to foresee all the evil he was to bring upon the earth by his disobedient act. That is to say, he, as created, was an *imperfect* being. Laws are made as man is weak and erring. And we *cannot impute* to God the defects of a bad mechanic, want of knowledge and skill. Man's reason does not accept the *other* explanation (no explanation at all - merely a confession of *ignorance*) that God's ways are mysterious. Why say at all that God made such a bad job? We don't thereby pull Him down from the position of the Creator and the Supreme Lord of the universe. In what sense He is the Creator is clearly explained in this book and is consistent with modern science. We cannot therefore say that man has an Adi - beginning. We simply deny that and say he is *anadi* (அநாதி) without beginning - eternal *i.e., more simply* that he exists. His existence is taken as a fact and admitting of no other explanation. So, his imperfection, *Anava Mala* and other *Malabandas* in union with him are also *anadi* - eternal. And the *illustrations* give some very apt analogies showing such mutual relationship and union. Paddy and Copper are the examples. A paddy grain appears as one; still, it is composed of the husk, bran, rice and the sprout, and all these are united together at the same time. Just as the physical covering of man *completely* hides his real self, so the husk may conceal the rice. There is one more thing which conceals the whiteness and purity of the rice (soul) and that is the dark bran (anava) more intimately

Sivagnana Botham of Meykanda Deva

connected with it. And then there is a sprout (Karma) but for which the grain will not germinate (attain births). And what is the use of the husk? Remove it, the seed will not germinate and grow into a plant (attain bodies) and when you want to get at the rice (the real self-soul) it helps by friction (by successive births - evolution) to remove the dark bran (*Anava-ignorance*.)

Take Copper again. As we find it imbedded in the bosom of a rock (God) it is a darksome ugly thing (man with his imperfections). What is it that makes it ugly, dims its real lustre? Its rust. When did it become covered with rust? It was always so. It is not a mere covering. The rust is in its very core. Was Copper (soul) derived from Gold (God)? No. Can its rust (anava) be removed and can it become Gold? We will see. Bring it into use (births) and by friction applied by the hand or tamarind (Maya) it brightens a little (becomes intelligent and active.) Lay it at rest, (resolution) the rust covers it again. And it is the Alchemist's belief that after an innumerable number of *Putams* (fire and friction) and when it had reached a certain kind of tone, a touch of the *Parisa Vedi* (*Alchemist*'s. stone) will turn it at once into Gold. And our belief is that after we had undergone a sufficient number of births, and we had reached *malaparibagam* (மலபரிபாகம்), God's grace (சக்திநி பாதம்) will touch and convert us into Himself. The Alchemist may or may not have succeeded in his life-long hope; at least there is no harm for us if we believe that we will reach perfection, Divine hood. At any rate, we are sure of reaching perfect manhood.

Cf. "கருமருவு குகையனைய காயத்தி எடுவுட்
களிம்புதோய் செம்பனையயான்
காண்டக விருக்கநீ ஞானவனன் மூட்டியே
கனிவுபெற வுள்ளுருக்கிப்
பருவம் தறிந்துநின் னருளான குளிகைகொடு
பரிசித்து வேதிசெய்து
பத்துமாற் றுத்தநுக மாக்கியே பணிகொண்ட
பகூழத்தை யென்சொல்லுகேன்·

"அருளுடைய பரமென்றோ அன்று தானே
யானுளனென் றும்மனக்கே யாண வாதி
பெருகுவினைக் கட்டென்று மென்னாற் கட்டிப்
பேசியதன் நெயருணூல் பேசிற் றன்றே."

— (Thayumanavar).

(*b*) The second illustration of the Sun and lotus shows that God is unchangeable - *Nirvikari* and impartial and just. His justice and mercy are not incompatible things. Out of His Supreme Love He lifts the souls from the deep darkness of Anava and puts them into the cycle of births, whereby they can obtain salvation sooner or later, according to their deserts, without any further interference on the part of God, showing us however the ways by which we can reach the goal. A physician can cure a man's bad sight, but if after that, he carelessly falls into a pit the physician cannot be blamed; or again a man has his sight - he can see with his eyes. But could he see without the light of the Sun? If we see wrong or do not carefully note the pitfalls, &c., and come to a mishap can we blame the Sun? We have our own intelligence to

Sivagnana Botham of Meykanda Deva

guide us, though the Divine Light surrounds us and enables us to use our intelligence. Man, therefore cannot shift on his moral responsibility to God.

3. This argument removes the doubt whether death is a final ending, - annihilation. The strongest point in the doctrine of this school is the principle that "nothing can come out of nothing" and that no effect can be produced without a cause, following the principle of conservation that nothing which is, can cease to be so. If the *Prapancha* (Body and mind) is an entity, it was established in the first Sutra that it was produced out of some primordial substance. It could not therefore cease to exist when it undergoes ordinary deaths. Deaths must necessarily therefore lead to re-births. So it is laid down that Births and Deaths are possible only when a thing is eternal. But what is that in it which brings about births and deaths. It is the Law of change - Continual change, Evolution. This eternal and continually changing ego undergoing births and re-births should not be confounded with the vaguely apprehended and feebly postulated ego of the southern Buddhists, a mere product of the Skandas, eking out some kind of continued existence, failing when the Skandas fail, and becoming annihilated also. We postulate also Nirvana and the word is used in such conjunctions as Nirvana Diksha, &c., but in what sense they are used will be shown later on. It does not mean annihilation.

(*a & b*). The illustrations explain how the soul and its inseparable and eternal body undergo birth, death, and rebirth. Man's visible body (*Sthula Sarira*) is only resolved into its cause *Sukshuma Sarira*, as water passes into invisible vapour. So the soul passing from its *Sthula Sarira* to its *Sukshuma Sarira* as illustrated in (*b*) experiences some pleasure or pain, as in sleep, the death of every day (Nithya Pralaya), the man experiences pleasant or unpleasant dreams, according to his experience of the previous day or days. When the soul had therefore eaten of its Karma in part and had received sufficient rest, its *Akamia Karma* induces it again to get a *Sthula Sarira*. Heaven or Hell are merely states or conditions of the soul's existence in *Sukshuma Sarira*. These have no local or space existence.

When the soul is in its *Sthula Sarira*, the faculties are active and receive full play. In its *Sukshuma state*, all the faculties are paralysed and inactive; though it is capable of certain experiences owing to the past experiences vaguely reproducing themselves. The dream condition is exactly its parallel. We don't remember all our days, experiences in sleep or dream; nor do we remember the numberless dreams that we dream in a night, when we wake up, unless it be very vivid or strong. Even when we are awake. We do not remember all our past actions, though sometimes they be a day old. Man is therefore not able to remember his life in a previous state or birth, through the changes in his mental and physical conditions and through his feeble powers of retentiveness.

4. It was already shown how God was in Adwaitha relation with the world. And this is not possible but for His Chit Sakti. And the relation of Himself to the Sakti is described as a *Samavaya* relation. This inseparable association is one and the same thing but we can regard the one in two different aspects. When we regard God in Himself apart from the world, He is Sivam, Pure Sat. When we regard Him in relation with the world, He is Sakti (Light, Energy, Chit.) When we regard the Sun as a great Luminous Body, we speak of him as the Sun; when we regard it as shining on the whole earth, we speak of its light. And how His relation with the

Sivagnana Botham of Meykanda Deva

world is what is called *Omnipresence*. This word though used by every religionist is not understood properly. Its true significance can only be understood when we understand what Adwaitham means. It is in fact synonymous with it. Inasmuch as there are some who understand Adwaitham as oneness, this word is used to mean that he is everything and that there could be nothing but him and there is no second thing as mind or matter. And the simple logic by which this position is established is stated in the following sentence.

"Were we to exclude the Omnipresent Principle form one mathematical point of the universe or from a particle of matter occupying any conceivable space, could we still regard it as infinite"? What does this mean? Omnipresence means a space relation. It is capable of extension, measurement. It can be viewed as a mathematical quantity.

If we suppose one unit of quantity occupies one unit of space, and the Omnipresent Principle and Matter being regarded in units of quantity, of course it is impossible for one unit of God and one unit of Matter to occupy one unit of space. This is mathematically and logically certain.

But is this position tenable? Are we to regard God as occupying space, a quantity, a thing with length and breadth *i. e.*, capable of extension i.e., as matter. But there are people who do so regard it; but they can't prove it by saying that God is Omnipresent. Then the argument will be in this form:-

God is matter.

Because God is Omnipresent. And Omnipresence means matter; which will be arguing in a vicious circle, there being really no major premise to this syllogism.

Even the broad distinction drawn between mind and matter is that the matter is what is capable of extension and mind is not. Can we therefore regard the Universal Mind as a thing capable of extension? Then what does this Omnipresence mean and imply? And how is, it God is Omnipresent? As was observed before, Omnipresence means a space relation, the notion of space is impossible apart from things co-existing. If we regard God as the Absolute and the Infinite, He could not be Omnipresent. Infinite space is a contradiction in terms. Omnipresence therefore implies a co-existing object. If God is a Principle diffusing and soaking through and through, it must diffuse and soak itself in another thing. If it fills what does it fill? If it fills itself then you must regard it as finite. As the Hindu Nyayikas put it, there could be no *Vyapakam*, (Omnipresence) all container, without things capable of Vyapti, (things filled). It is therefore established God is Omnipresent and His Presence is felt in other things and that God is not space, nor matter, nor the universe. Then how does He fill the universe? According to the text it is by His Chit Sakti or Gnana Sakti. God is all Gnanam. He is Gnana Mayam, and Gnanam is not space nor Matter nor Malam. And it is therefore possible to fill one unit of space with one unit of matter and one of Gnanam or God. He is then neither one with matter nor apart nor different from it. It is in this way He is Omnipresent. It is His great *Chaitanyam* that fills His body (Souls, and Mala or Matter). It is in us He dwells and it is in this sense and sense alone "that ye are the temple of God."

Sivagnana Botham of Meykanda Deva

"அறவையேன் மனமே, கோயிலாக்கொண்டு ஆண்டு
அளவிலா ஆனந்தமருளி."

(Manicka Vachaka). In the same way as our Sakti - intelligence fills our body, so God's Sakti (Maha Chaitanyam) pervades our souls and lightens our darkness (உள்ளத்தொளிக்கின்ற ஒளி) and He is then truly "Our Father in Heaven" 'whom' we are cognisant with us, in our heart and Spiritual consciousness.' If otherwise we are God, how could God be itself cognisant of itself in its heart and spiritual consciousness. In fact consciousness is a thing which cannot be predicated of the Absolute. Of course, we can hardly conceive how mind fills matter and from want of the adequate idea, an inadequate word is used; Omnipresence is not at all the best word to be used to bring out the idea and it is this improper use of the word which has caused all the mistake and confusion; as many another word has done.

The illustration states a paradox. If He is all-pervading He cannot be one, and if He is two, He cannot be all-pervading. All that is meant is, He cannot be regarded as a finite being, a thing capable of extension, &c., He is all in all. He is all and not all. Our intelligence and action is nothing when compared with His Supreme Gnanam. We are entirely subordinate to Him. Before His Supreme Presence, every matter is nothing. It is like His property. It is in this sense our Thayumanavar exclaims:-

"எல்லாம்உன் அடிமையே; எல்லாம்உன் உடைமையே;
எல்லாம்உன் னுடையசெயலே."

Compare also the definition of *Paripuranam* (பரிபூரணம்) given in Ozhivilodukkam

"உதியா துளதாகி ஓங்கிப்பே ராமல்
அதிதுக் குமங்குறைந்தா காமற் - பதையாத
ஆகாய முங்காலும் போல வசைவற்ற
தேகாண் பரிபூ ரணம்."

It has no origin. It is *Sat*. It transcends all the 36 *tatwas*. It is unchangeable (*Achalam*.) It is *adisukshuma* (the least of the least,) as it is in everything and yet out of it. It could not be lessened nor increased (*Akandaharam* - Infinite.) It is immoveable in relation with the universe as the *Akas* is connected with air in perfect calm. This then is *Paripuranam* - Omnipresence.

III

THIRD SUTRA.

ON THE EXISTENCE OF SOUL.

Sutra: - It rejects every portion of the body as not being itself; It says my body; it is conscious of dreams; it exists in sleep without feeling pleasure or pain or movements; it knows from others; This is the soul which exists in the body formed as a machine from *Maya*.

Commentary.

This treats of Atma Prakasa and consists of seven arguments.

First Argument.

Choornika: - An intelligent soul exists, as its intelligence is exercised when it says "this is not the soul, this is not the soul."

Varthikam: - As there exists something after it rejects everything else as not being the soul, it is established that this something is the soul.

Udarana: - Standing in intimate and inseparable connection with each and every part of the body and its organs, an intelligence of the form of *Sri Panchatchara* is found to exist which is not one or other of these. That Thou art. Thou art not *Maya*, with which thou art united, as it only enables thy understanding to shine better as the eye-glasses make the eye see better. Thou art neither the Supreme Being (Tat Param) who is above thyself and Maya. Thou art different from both.

Second Argument

Choornika. - As the phrase "my body" is used in a separate possessive sense, there is a soul different from the body.

Varthikam: - As something exists apart when it says 'this is my arm' 'this is my leg' as when it speaks of my town, and my house. It is established that this something is the soul.

Udarana: - As thou speakest of thy wife and thy house as thine and as identical with thyself, so thou speakest of thy hands and thy feet and thy impression and sensation, as though they are not different from you. If examined deeply, thou wilt find the body, arms, &c. to be different from thyself.

Third Argument

Choornika: - As he understands all the five different sensations, he is different from all the five senses which can only feel each a particular sensation.

Sivagnana Botham of Meykanda Deva

Varthikam: - As among the five senses, one cannot feel what another can feel, and as there exists something which feels all the five classes of sensations by means of all the five senses, it is established that this something is the soul.

Udarana: - If there is something which understands the actions of all the five senses in the body which are moved by *Sri Panchatchara* and of which when experiencing the sensations, one sense does not feel what another sense feels, that something thou art. As these senses except feeling each differently have no thought that they feel, understand that thou art not one of them.

Fourth Argument

Choornika: - As it passes from the dream conditions into the waking state, there exists a soul different from the body in the dream condition.

Varthikam: - As something experiences in the waking state that it had dreams in sleep, it is established that this something is the soul.

Udarana: - When, in sleep, the senses which are alive in the body, lose their action and the body loses all its external actions, thou enterest another body, (*Sukshuma Sarira*) inside thy own, in dream and undergoes other experiences of sight, hearing and the like, pleasure, and pain and the like and then changest it for the visible body (*Sthula Sarira*) when waking. Thou art not therefore the *Sukshuma Sarira*; Thou art different.

Fifth Argument

Choornika: - As the body has no feelings or movements in profound sleep, though respiration in kept up, the soul is different from the respiratory organ (Pranavayu).

Varthikam: - In profound sleep (when all the functions of the body except respiration are suppressed), feelings of pleasure and pain and movements are absent in the body; and in the waking state, when all the faculties are in working order, these feelings and movements are present. It is therefore established that something (which thus suppresses the faculties or brings them into play, causing the absence or presence of the feelings and movements) is the soul.

Udarana: - (In profound sleep) the body, which has cognition of the world, losing it, has no feeling of pleasure or pain and no movements, though the breath (respiration) fully plays. Hence, there is an intelligence which has such perception other than breath. Understand that when the soul is active in the body, it has such feelings and movements.

Sixth Argument

Choornika: - The soul becomes conscious of one thing when it forgets another. Therefore, the soul is different from Hara, whose consciousness is not subject to such change.

Varthikam: - As it can only understand when taught by its Guru that it is different from God whose understanding is perfect, it is established that this is the soul (and not God).

Sivagnana Botham of Meykanda Deva

Udarana: - When becoming conscious of objects, it only apprehends one at a time, and when proceeding to apprehend another, becomes unconscious of what it knew before, and when it undergoes the five avasthas it becomes perfectly unconscious of everything. What is it which so apprehends? It is not Intelligence (*Arivu*). If the truth seeker examines, it is the soul whose understanding becomes identical with what it becomes united to.

Seventh Argument

Choornika: - The soul is different from all the various tatwas as each is called by a separate name.

Varthikam: - It is established that the soul is different from the body, as each of the five senses instead of being called soul receives each a different name.

Udarana: - If the intelligence is the result of the conjunction of the bodily organs and (senses) these, on examination, resolve themselves into the *Tatwas* which begin with *Kala* and end with earth, and these are products of *Maya* which earth, and these are products of Maya which is not permanent (changeable or destructible.) If, after understanding attentively the nature of intelligence, this combination is examined, it is simply the body (*Sthula*) and (*Sukshuma*) which is to the soul what the lamplight is to the eye. Hence the soul or intelligence is different from the body.

NOTES

This Sutra is a remarkable example of condensation of thought and brevity of expression. This contains 7 arguments on a most important subject and yet there is only a word or two to express each argument and there are not more than 20 words in Tamil or 14 words in Sanskrit. The first Sutra established from the fact of the objective universe and its undergoing evolution, the existence of Sat. In the next Sutra the nature of Chit by which this evolution is brought about and which is all Love is explained. Now God need not be active and be all loving, if nobody is to be benefited by it. He could not desire anything for Himself, as He is "வேண்டுதல் வேண்டாமையிலான்" (has no likes nor dislikes). Every act of His must be construed as *Para-prayochanam* and not *Swaprayochanam*. We have therefore to postulate a separate entity as Soul which requires the support of the Supreme Intelligence and Love. This Sutra therefore proceeds to the proof of its existence.

1. The first argument is directed against Suniyavadis according to whom there is no Atma at all. The subject though it identifies itself with every part of the objective body, organs and sensations yet it exercises its sense of difference and distinguishes itself from one and all of these. Therefore, that which so discriminates could not be a not-entity. This discriminating subject is the Soul of *Atma*. Even if we were to think we do not exist, the very thinking so, proves the existence of the thinking beings. The illustration further enjoins a caution that this thinking intelligence, being no other than Atma is not to be confounded with Divine intelligence, when we see it is not Maya or objective consciousness. The Atma occupies a place different from the other two *i.e.*, a middle position. God is Sat; Maya is Asat; hence Atma is

Sivagnana Botham of Meykanda Deva

called Satasat (சதசத்து). The author of Ozhivilodukkam calls it *Ali Arivu* (அலியறிவு - Hermaphrodite intelligence) comparing the Divine Arivu to male and the Maya Arivu to female intelligence. Though all these are intelligences, they are of different orders. There is a dependence of the lower intelligence on the higher and when viewed from the stand-point of the higher, the lower ceases to exist as it were, the latter becomes Asat. Maya is Sat, but as compared with Atma, it is Asat. Atma is sat but as compared with God is *Asat*; Maya could not be compared with anything lower, nor God (*Sat*) with anything higher. So, these latter occupy extremes *Asat* and *Sat* and the middle one is called *Sadasat*, partaking of the nature of both and not being both. When it identifies itself with Maya, (as in man) it is hardly distinguishable from Maya and when it becomes identified with Sat, its presence cannot also be seen. So it is an *Ali* (Hermaphrodite).

One other distinction between *Sat* and *Sadasat* is that Sat is intelligence that induces Perception (காட்டும் அறிவு or அறிவிக்கும் அறிவு) or Light that removes darkness and the latter is Intelligence that perceives after the darkness is removed by *Sat* (காணும் or அறியும் அறிவு).

The relation of God, Atma and Maya is illustrated by the following analogy. Atma is the eye which is affected by a general disability and a particular defect. It cannot see in darkness nor when its eye sight is defective. God is the Sun, the dispeller of darkness, thereby giving light to the eye and other objects and enabling it to perceive. Maya is like the eye glasses which afford temporary relief to defective sight. By continued use of the glasses (births) and by a touch of the Surgeon's lancet (God's Grace or Arul Sakti) the defective eye sight (Anavamala) may be permanently cured. But the defective eye sight could not be cured by the Sun however powerful it may shine, and it shines ever before and after the eye sight is cured. And yet at no moment could you compare the light of the eye to the light of the sun, the one is the dispeller of darkness and the other is subject to darkness inherently. *Sri Panchatchara* is synonymous with Pranava. See further treatment of the subject in the subsequent chapters. Cf. Thayumanavar.

"ஐந்துபுலன் ஐம்பூதம் கரணமாதி
அடுத்தகுண மத்தனையும் அல்லை அல்லை
இந்த உடல் அறிவு அறியாமையு நீ யல்லை
யாதொன்று பற்றினதன் இயல்பாய் நின்று
பந்தமறும் பளிங்கனைய சித்து நீ யுன்
பக்குவங் கண்டறிவிக்கும் பான்மையேம் யாம்."

2. This is an argument gathered from a habit of speech to prove that the Soul is different from the body as against the *Theganma Vadis*. The different forms of speech I and mine involve a difference between the non-Ego (body) and the Ego and asserts the separate existence of the Ego. Such usages as 'I am the body'; 'I am the leg or arm,' &c., are not in existence.

3. This argument is against regarding the soul as identical with the five external senses. Each sense stands apart and cannot feel a different class of sensations. So the Soul can neither

Sivagnana Botham of Meykanda Deva

be one nor all of them. Even when the sensations are experienced, there is simply the feeling present and no thought of any such feeling. The eye sees no doubt, but it does not think that it sees. This is of course the distinction between subjective thought and objective feeling. The objective feeling or object is not the subject mind or Atma.

4. This argument is against the view that *Sukshuma Sarira* is itself the *Atma*. That it is not so is proved by the fact of the Soul passing in the waking state into the *Sthula Sarira* remembering its experiences in sleep and remembering them not clearly even.

In fact, it is in the *Sthula Sarira*, all the faculties are present and in full play; and in the *Sukshuma Sarira* 10 of the Tatwas (5 elements and 5 senses) are wanting. In dream, there is merely reproduction of ideas as determined by the previous Karma (experiences) and without the command of reason or will. This sensorium and blind reproduction is not the subject. It can be so, if in that condition the Soul is in its full working order.

5. Nor is the Soul in its full working order and undergoing movements, feelings, &c., in dead sleep and hence the respiratory organ is not the Atma. In *Jakratha*, respiratory function is working but in conjunction with other organs, external and internal senses, and certain sequences follow, feelings and actions. If the first is the sole cause or Atma, then we must eliminate other antecedents and see if the sequences still continue. In *Sukshupthi*, the other antecedents are absent and the respiratory function is the sole function present and it is not accompanied by the sequences. This is the inductive method of elimination of antecedents as causes which are not followed by the same effects. This same method is also used in the last argument.

6. The law of human consciousness as here stated is the same as that postulated by Dr. Bain, "change is essential to consciousness." Unless we change our thought to another, our consciousness of the thought ceases. To be conscious of the next we must forget the present. So, the Tamil axiom is stated as "நினைப்புண்டேல் மறப்புண்டாம்" "When we are conscious we are also subject to forgetfulness." When we continue to think of a particular object or idea for a time and do not change it, we in fact do not continue conscious of it. Our mind becomes incapable of thinking, owing to its inherent weakness. Man's intelligence therefore is weak or changing; and it is this which distinguishes it from God who is all Intelligence, who is cognizant of all at the same time. One other distinction is Human Intelligence requires to be taught, improved and developed; it is imperfect and needs the support of a Perfect Intelligence.

7. This argument sums up all the previous arguments, and points out one distinction between the bodily senses, Sukshuma and Karma Sariras which are all products of Maya, and the Soul. The distinction is that whereas these products of matter are ever changeable and changing and hence called *Asat* or false, the soul is unchangeable and hence called *Sat*. This sat however becomes Asat when in union with Asat or Maya and Sat when in union with the True Sat or God and hence it is called *Sadasat*. The definition of Asat is given in the first *Varthika* of the sixth Sutra. It does not mean non-existent, but one perceivable in one aspect or objective attitude of the soul and not perceivable in the subjective attitude of the soul.

Sivagnana Botham of Meykanda Deva

This finishes the chapter on proof. I have already pointed out that Maya (Cosmic Matter) and Anava (Imperfection in nature) are taken as facts and not capable of further explanation or resolution into any other cause, and that matter undergoes evolution, and that there is some method in this and this method is determined by Karma (Law of Causation.) And matter not being capable of Evolution itself and the individual Ego not being able to determine the Evolution, we require a Superior Force, a Grand Energy and this is the Unknowable. Its relation with mind and matter is *Adwaitha* and its Omnipresence is brought about by its *Maha Chaitanyam*. The reason for separately postulating a soul is then shown and this soul could not be confounded with *Buvana* and *Bhoga*, and is proved to be other than the body, the five senses, and *Sukshuma Sarira* and *Karana Sarira*; That is, it is different from Maya as well as from God. one group of Phenomena or faculties have been omitted from the consideration of these questions and that is, the four internal senses, *Manas, Buddhi, Chittam* and *Ahankaram* and these four answer to the Mind of the Western Philosophers. These are also shown to be distinct from the soul and as the subject requires a fuller treatment it is discussed in a separate Sutra. It will be seen from what follows that these occupy a middle position between the Soul and the objective Phenomena (*Thanu*, external senses, and *Buvana*, and *Bhoga*); and there is thus involved a triple division of man, as soul, mind and animal life (body). As between mind and body, body is object (Asat) and mind is sat; as between the soul and the other two, the last two are objective (Asat) and the soul the subject (Sat). As between God and Soul and the rest, God is the True subject (Sat) and soul and the rest are objective (Asat) This relationship is discussed in the subsequent chapters and must be borne in mind. It is a point for the Scientific Inquirer to consider if the proof adduced in this chapter is sufficient and convincing, or if the statement is taken as a mere theory or hypothesis (and in these grand question it is not possible to arrive at more than a true hypothesis) whether it is a true hypothesis i.e., whether it explains all the phenomena of human existence and satisfies all human aspiration or whether it omits any facts unexplained and contradicts any facts of our existence. It is also a point worth notice that in the elucidation of these principles, nothing is made a matter of mystery - no real difficulty left unexplained by being consigned to the realms of the mysterious, and language is not used to puzzle man and baffle argument. When once proof is attempted, so far as the human mind is capable of grasping and proving these things, one must confine oneself to strictly human logical tests, and if the theory fails on the application of these tests the theory must be condemned by human reason. If after all the trouble taken to postulate a theory, adduce proof &c. a man is going to plead his own ignorance and God's mysterious ways, it would be far better for him to confess his ignorance at the beginning and attempt no explanation at all.

CHAPTER - II. LAKSHANAVIAL

IV - FOURTH SUTRA

OF THE SOUL IN ITS RELATION TO THE ANDHAKARANA

Sutra: - The soul is not one of the Andakarana. It is not conscious when it is in conjunction with Anavamala. It becomes conscious only when it meets the Andakarana, just as a king understands through his ministers. The relation of the soul to the five Avastha is also similar.

Commentary

This also treats of the nature of the soul and it consists of three arguments.

First Argument:

Choornika: - The *Andhakarana* have no activity except when in conjunction with the soul. Hence there is a soul distinct from the Andhakarana.

Varthikam: - As the *Andhakaranas* are only intelligent (chit) when viewed in relation to the subordinate *Tatwas* but are non-intelligent (*Achit*) when viewed in relation to the soul, it is established that the soul is not one of the *Andhakaranas* namely *Manas, Buddhi, Chittam* and *Ahankaram*.

Udarana: - (*a*) *Manas* and other *Andhakaranas* have perception of permanent sensations. The soul perceives the product of the perception by the *Buddhi* after such *mental* perceptions. These perceptions by *Manas* and *Buddhi* reach the soul as the waves rising in the sea reach the shore. As the *Andhakaranas* are different from the permanent sensations, so the soul is different from the *Andhakarana*.

(*b*) While perceiving so, the soul as *Chittam* considers; as *Manas* it doubts; as *Andhakarana*, it wrongly concludes; as *Buddhi* it determines properly. As it thus apprehends differently when it is united to each, it is different from them, just as the sun, though marking the divisions of time, is different from it.

(*c*) The letter 'A' is the symbol of *Ahankaram*; 'U' that of *Buddhi*; 'M' that of *Manas*; *Vinthu* that of *Chittam*; and *Natham* which is inseparable from all these letters, is the symbol of the soul. The five letters constitute *Pranava*; when examined, consciousness arises when the soul and *andakarana* meet, just as the tides rise and fall during the conjunction of the sun and the Moon.

(*d*) *Iswara* and *Sadasiva* are the deities respectively of *Vinthu* and *Natham*; *Brahma, Vishnu* and *Rudra* are deities respectively of 'A,' 'U,' and 'M'.

Sivagnana Botham of Meykanda Deva

Second Argument

Choornika: - The soul cannot see, being shrouded by the *mala*.

Varthikam: - It is established that the soul cannot understand when it is solely in conjunction with its inherent *mala* (*Anava*), as this *mala* is something which darkens the soul's light or intelligence.

Udarana: - The soul will not know anything, unless it receives the light through its body caused by *Maya*, as the eye apprehends objects by the light of the lamp. *Anavamala* exists in the soul eternally, becoming one with it and concealing its luster as does the firewood conceal the heat or fire present in it.

Third Argument

Choornika: - The soul undergoes five *Avasthas*.

Varthikam: - As the soul is in a formless (*Arupa*) tatwa form and shrouded by the *Mala*, it is established that the soul undergoes five *Avasthas*, namely, *Jakra, Swapna, Sushupti, Thuriya*, and *Thuriyatheetha*.

Udarana: - (*a*) In the *Jakra Avastha* of the soul, when it is in the region of the forehead, it has 35 active organs including the 10 external senses. In its *Swapna Avastha*, when in the region of the throat, it has 25 organs excluding the 10 external organs. In the *Sushupti Avastha*, when in the region of the heart, it has 3 organs including *Chittam*. In *Thuriya Avastha*, when in the region of the navel, it has only two, namely *Purusha* and *Pranavayu*; In *Thuriyatheetha Avastha*, when in the region of *Mulathara*, it is pure *Purusha* having none of these organs.

(*b*) The soul, which in *Jakra avastha* is in the region of the forehead, undergoes all the five *avasthas* in the same region. That is to say, it becomes conscious of each perception through each of the organs and, at the same time, becomes separated from them. *Sutta Avastha* are like these five in number.

NOTES

Andhakarana is a generic word, signifying all the internal senses, but they more particularly mean as here, *Manas, Buddhi, Chitta* and *Ahankara*. The proof of the proposition that the soul is not one of the *Andhakarana* is given in the Varthika and udaranas. In dead sleep (*Sushupthi*) where the internal senses are at rest, the soul is not conscious. It becomes conscious only when the *Anthakarana* become once more active. When the soul is in *Sushupti*, it is in conjunction only with *Anava Mala* and performing respiratory function. This last function is the watchman who guards the innermost portals of the Palace of the King (Soul) when it is in perfect solitude. The *Avasthas* are merely the conditions of the soul when it is in relation with all the external and internal senses or with only some of them or none at all.

Sivagnana Botham of Meykanda Deva

1. The *Choornika* furnishes the first proof which is amplified in the *Varthika*. The internal senses are active; you lift your Ego to its own place as in *Yoga*, the *Andhakarana* become dead and inactive, thus showing that the Atma is not one of the *Andhakaranas*.

The distinction is drawn in the following manner.

The *Andhakaranas* are the faculties of perception and reason. They perceive and reason but are not conscious that they perceive and reason. This latter function is performed by the True Ego, Atma.

The four *Andhakaranas* are distinguished; among them, wise *Chittam* takes an impression presented by the senses and considers what it is. It cannot know that it so considers.

Manas takes such an impression, and double whether it is or is not this or that. It cannot know that it so doubts.

Ahankara ventures boldly that the impression is such and such. It cannot know that it so ventures.

Buddhi determines properly that the impression is this or that. It cannot know that it so determines.

(*a*) The *Andhakaranas* are divided into two classes as remarked above.

Manas, *Chitta*, and *Ahankara* are merely faculties of perception and they perceive permanent sensations and the language of the text is remarkable as "மன்று புலன்கள்" exactly mean permanent sensations. *Buddhi* is the faculty of reason involving the sense of agreement and difference among such impressions. The product of this faculty is what is brought to the cognizance of the soul. The first three ministers merely gather statistics and prepare them. The Chief Minister, *Buddhi* compares the statistics and draws his conclusions and formulates the proposition to the King (Soul).

As the waves are stirred by the winds, the senses affect the *Andhakarana*.

(*b*) Another distinction is that the four andakarana are four different functions, one not capable of performing the function of another or all the rest. That which stands above, cognizant of all the four, is the soul.

(*c*) It was before observed that the soul was of the form of *Sri Panchatchara* and the latter was stated as synonymous with *Pranava*. The symbol of *Vinthu* is a circle and that of *Natham* is a line. These two in fact, constitute the *Pranava* symbol – or ௨ and the latter will be been is the same as *Pillayar shuli*; no Tamil man will begin the smallest piece of writing without prefixing *Pillayar shuli*. The significance being forgotten, it is thought of as a sectarian symbol, and the bigoted among *Vaishnavas* to whom the *Pranava* is as important, begin now to use ஸ்ரீ instead. Why it is called *Pillayar shuli* is, because God, Ganesha, represents Pure Sat, Brahm and the elephant Head is the Pranava symbol. Cf. the popular Tamil couplet.

Sivagnana Botham of Meykanda Deva

பிரணவப்பொருளாம் பெருந்தகை ஐங்கரன்
சரண அற்புதமலர் தலைக்கணிவோமே.

The popular Sanskrit slokas in praise of Ganesha also describe Him as *Pranava Sworupi*. The illustration contained in this stanza is a beautiful one.

(*d*) This contains another explanation of *Pranava*. *Sivam* was first stated as True *Sat* or *Brahm*. I have shown that the form of Ganesha shows Him to represent True Sat or Brahm. The very name of Subramanya signifies that He is True Brahm. The word Uma meaning Sakti is composed of u, m and a, *i.e.*, Om manifested. So, these different words or mantras are different modes of expressing the same principle, the True *Sat*, in symbol, sound and language. So, *Om, Sri Panchatchara, Ganesha mantra, Subramanya mantra* and *Devi mantra* are mere equivalents and denote the *Samashti Pranava*; when analyzed *i.e.*, regarded as *Vyashti*, it becomes divided into *Natham, Vinthu*, a, u, and m. 'a' represents creation or origin as its place is the place or origin of all sounds. 'u' or 'oo' represents *sthithi*, as, when after pronouncing 'a' we bring it to a stand for an instant by converging the lips, 'u' is formed; when we close our mouths after pronouncing 'a' and 'u,' 'm' is formed and hence it represents *Samharam. Binthu* and *Natham* are the form and sound of these letters.

2. This explains that man's intelligence only receives play and brightness and is capable of infinite improvement, when brought in contact with human body, by getting frequent births. That is, by evolution alone, man gets himself perfected.

3. I have not seen any objection to regarding the Soul as a separate entity more formidable that this, viz.

"If so, while I am in my objective state of consciousness, my Ego is something existing as a real entity in the physical body itself. How is it possible to transfer the same to the astral body? Then, again, it has also to be transferred to the *Karana Sarira*. We shall find a still greater difficulty in transferring this entity to the Logos itself; and you may depend upon it that unless a man's individuality or Ego can be transferred to the Logos, immortality is only a name." This objection which is stated with so much confidence will, on examination, be found to be groundless. In the first place, it is not shown, how it is not possible to effect the transference from one Avastha to another under this theory and that it is possible under the objector's theory. Besides, the difficulty is more in the language employed, than in actual fact. And it is, often, in our experience what a fruitful source of error is the inadequate language we employ, in describing laws of thought. The objector speaks of the transfer from one body to another. On the premises already laid down in the preceding Sutras and on the view of the Avasthas as discussed in this argument, it will be apparent that there will be no transfer at all. The atma does not fly from the *Sthula Sarira* into the *Sukshuma* or astral body and leaving this into the *Karana Sarira*. It did not enter any new cosmic body at any one time. Its connection with Maya is eternal. And the law of mental evolution or evolution of subjective consciousness corresponds exactly to the evolution of objective consciousness. The human mind cannot evolve unless there is a corresponding evolution in its body. A pure disembodied mind or Atma is not recognized by this school. In the human as well as in the freed state (Moksha) it is

Sivagnana Botham of Meykanda Deva

connected with matter and between matter and God, the Atma is supported like a piece of iron between two magnets, the one pulling it higher and the other pulling it lower. And in the human state, the iron is in closest contact with the lower magnet, and in the Moksha with the Higher Magnet. In Moksha, the power of maya to undergo births alone is destroyed, by the Karma having been eaten up, just as a seed of grain loses its power of germination in the granary of the ant, by the sprout being nibbled off or by some other process. In human evolution, however, we find both the object and subject being evolved together and there could be no evolution of the one without the evolution of the other. In its original condition, what is here called *Thuriyatheetha* condition, the atma is pure Purusha without consciousness of any sort, its body also being altogether undeveloped. This is the stage before evolution had commenced. The atma has no consciousness, no intelligence and no movements of any sort. In the next condition (*Thuriya avastha*) evolution had been started, we have the first beginning of life, *Purusha*, in a living breathing body, without consciousness or any manifestation of any other faculties. They (mind and body) are evolved a step further in the *Sushupthi avastha*, and we have the first beginning of consciousness; and as such the faculty of *Chittam* is evolved in addition; and the objective body is then called *Karana Sarira*. A step further we arrive at *Swapna avastha*, where all the faculties (objective consciousness) except the 10 external senses (*Gnana and Karma Indriyas*) are fully developed and the objective body is called *Sukshuma* or astral body. In the final stage of evolution, where man's consciousness has been fully developed, all the 36 *tatwas* formed of *Maya*, have been also fully developed; this is the *Jakra avastha*, and the body is the *Sthula* body. In this account of human evolution, there is no transference really. Similarly when the atma and its body undergo resolution, subjective and objective consciousness ceases little by little or is drawn in as it were, just as a spider or tortoise draws all its legs and organs into itself and rolls itself into a mass and becomes dead to all appearance. In fact, like a revolving prism of many sides, the attitude of the atma alone changes and this change of attitude or avastha is brought about, as, in the language of the text, it is in a formless (*Arupa*) *Tatwa* form enshrouded by *mala i.e.*, not being made of matter but being chit itself and encased in matter. These five avasthas and their bodies are divided into three states *Kevala*, *Sakala* and *Sutta*. The *Kevala* state is the original state before evolution and described in the text of this sutra 'சகசமலத்துணராது' (It is not conscious when it is in conjunction with *Anavamala*). The *Sakala* state is described in the next sutra (V) and in the next one (VI) the Sutta state is treated of.

Having met a few of the most formidable objections taken to this view of the Siddhanta school, let me here state a few of the objections to the Idealistic view for which a rational answer is not yet forthcoming. Evolving Logos and *Mulaprakriti* (matter) from *Brahm* (*Sat*), why don't you apply the law of causation and conservation of energy, and say otherwise that, *Logos* and matter are not *Brahm*, and why do you throw a veil between *Logos* and *Brahm*, and why do you say also that matter is not '*Sat*' but *Asat*, and why should the one energy or Chaitanyam or Sakti of the Logos subdivide itself and form into different monads and acquire Karma, and become evil, and corrupt and bring sin and sorrow into this earth? If Atma is not a particle of this *Chit* but a mere reflection or shadow, how could a mere shadow become individualized and clothe with thought and action? And why should this shadow work out its own salvation? Will it not disappear when the substance is itself resolved. And in the same way

Sivagnana Botham of Meykanda Deva

as the Logos manifested itself in various bodies, as the sun in various pots of water, cannot the Logos itself gather up its lost energies or cannot the energy pass into the Logos as soon as the body dies, just as the sun's reflection ceases as soon as the water pot is broken? With what grace can the objection be stated that unless the man's individuality is transferred into the Logos itself, immortality is only a name, when for no reason or end, the human monad is evolved from Logos, and when there is an equal chance for the individual attaining immortality to evolve again as a human monad?

Sivagnana Botham of Meykanda Deva

V

FIFTH SUTRA.

ON THE RELATION OF GOD, SOUL AND BODY.

Sutra: - The senses while perceiving the object cannot perceive themselves or the soul; and they are perceived by soul. Similarly, the soul while perceiving cannot perceive itself (while thinking cannot think thought) and God. It is moved by the Arul Sakti of God, as the magnet moves the iron, while Himself remains immoveable or unchangeable.

Commentary

This treats of the way in which God renders good or actuates the souls and consists of two arguments.

First Argument

Choornika: - The *Tatwas* act with the aid of the soul.

Varthikam: - It is established that the five senses perceive only as the instruments of the soul, as they can perceive nothing when not acting together with the soul.

Udarana: - The soul has regal sway over the five senses; these are not conscious of the soul and its sway, and the soul itself will have no consciousness except through the five Senses; but if the soul itself is not active the eye though seeing cannot see, and the ear though hearing, cannot hear.

Second Argument

Choornika: - The souls understand with the aid of Hara.

Varthikam: - As the soul cannot perceive itself, in the same way, the five senses cannot feel except with the aid of the soul, it is established that the soul also perceives with the aid of God.

Udarana: - (a) Thou who hast even forgotten the text of the Veda which says that the world (animate and inanimate) becomes developed in the presence of *Siva*, understand that the soul knows (the world) only according to its *Karma* with the light of *Siva*. As all *Asat* is *sunya*, He cannot experience *Asat*.

(b) Just as the stars which lose their individual light in the light of the sun and yet do not become the sun itself, so the soul receiving impressions. From all the five senses with the aid of God who is the only Truth, becomes indistinguishable and inseparable from Him (without becoming one or different from Him.)

(c) The *Arul* of *Isa* exists eternally with Him. It is His *Sakti*. Without Him, *Sakti* does not exist; and without *Sakti*, He cannot be. *Hara* (and His *Sakti*) appear as one to the *gnanis*, as the sun and its light appear as one to the eye.

Sivagnana Botham of Meykanda Deva

NOTES

This Sutra points out the essential limitation of all human senses, faculties, and the soul. The power of each is limited to knowing or perceiving the lower one and it cannot perceive itself or the higher faculty, and one faculty cannot perform the functions of another. The external and internal senses and the soul are therefore placed in an ascending order. Of these the highest, the soul can only perceive and know what is subordinate to itself. It cannot know itself nor know God. It is on this analogy and for this reason that God is imperceivable by the human senses and inconceivable by the human mind or soul; and it will be seen further that the soul cannot see God at any time by its own powers and that even the Yogi sees nothing but a figment of his own brain.

Not only are these human powers limited in their nature but there exists an interdependence of the lower over the higher. In the last sutra, it was shown that the soul does not become conscious till the Andakarana are evolved from matter; and it is here shown that the Andakarana themselves will not act unless the soul influences them and act together; and that the Andakarana have no independent action. And it is further seen that the higher consciousness exists or even predominates when the lower ones' ceases. That which stands therefore to the soul as the soul stands towards mind, is God, 'முற்றறிவன்', Perfect Intelligence பேறறிவன் 'Supreme intelligence' or as described in the next sutra 'Siva Sat' or 'Chit Sat.' And herein consists the most important distinction between God and man, and which entitles this school of philosophers to call themselves *Asthika* and all the rest (theistic and atheistic) *Nasthika*. In the latter theistic schools, their ideal of God is a purely personal or human one i.e., man raised to a God, or as in the idealistic school, God is brought down to the level of man, in either of which cases, the conception of God does not soar higher than that of man and the true ideal of God is never reached. Coming to the distinction noted above God and man do not differ in mere place or quantity or quality or in degree of power, strength or intelligence. It is not the same order of being differing merely in the amount of strength and intelligence. Man, is not a particle of God, so that the requisite number of particles of human souls will make up one God. Put thus, the idea is absurd enough, yet one finds thousands of people believing in the theory. The real difference is that God and man belong each to a different order or plane or existence. Just as we ascend from the plane of objective consciousness to the plane of subject or mental consciousness and just as we ascend from the latter to the consciousness of true subject or soul, also do we ascend from the latter consciousness to True Sat or God. The base of the lower rests upon the higher but not as effect and cause. Such expressions as உயிருக்குயிர் (Life of life) அறிவுக்கறிவு (Intelligence of Intelligences) express the relation clearly and yet we find these expressions freely used by Idealistic philosophers without any meaning. According to the latter school, God will be an அறிவு (Intelligence) and not an அறிவுக்கறிவு (Intelligence of Intelligences). When Siddhanthins use the expression "எல்லாம் சிவன்செயல்" "All actions are God's actions," they are also misunderstood often times, and the expression simply means that God is He who sustains our very being and actions as He vivifies our intelligence. Though there is dependence of the soul on God in respect of its Itcha (will) Gnana (Intelligence) and Kriya (action) yet the souls self-action and responsibility is not destroyed. For instance, when I move my arm, not only is my volition and energy (Itcha and Kriya Sakti) brought into play but the same action is sustained by and is possible only in the presence of the supreme energy (Kriya Sakti) of God. When I think also, Gnana Sakti of God is also brought into play. Only when God works, He does not work as we do. As the 1st illustration to the second argument points out, His presence produces these effects (சந்நிதிக்கே ஐந்து தொழிலாம்). And even then, He does not suffer any change as pointed out in the Sutra. Analogous are these. All the actions of the human body are supported and aided in the end

Sivagnana Botham of Meykanda Deva

by the Force of Gravity which is one and uniform, and yet in ordinary language we do not recognize its power, though a scientific account of all the causes must include it as well. Similarly, all our visual perceptions are aided by the Sun's Light which is one and uniform. Yet I say merely 'I see.' Accordingly, the ignorant do not recognize and feel the Power of the Lord, but the wise recognizing this Power, try to realize and feel it by withdrawing more and more from themselves and bringing themselves more and more into contact or rapport with Him, aided thereto by His *Arul Sakti*. And the last illustration appropriately discusses the nature of this *Arul Sakti*. The approximation of man to God results in the end in adwaitha relation as described in the 2nd illustration. In day light, the light of the star is completely lost to all sight and yet not lost. The light of the star blends with and becomes indistinguishable from the light of the Sun. Its identity is lost and not itself. There is no annihilation of the soul but its individuality or Egoism is lost, its Karma having been eaten. This is Moksha or Nirvana, according to the *Saiva Siddhantin*. Then and then alone will its action, if it has any, be in reality that of the Lord. The subject is further discussed in the next Sutra.

The limitation of the human intelligence is thus described in Sivagnana Siddhi, "The soul understands with the aid of the Supreme Intelligence as it understands through some sense or other, forgets what it has learnt, learns from others, is not conscious of itself, does not understand of itself."

On the other hand, God is described as '*Swa-Para-Prakasam*' 'He who is self-luminous and illumines others.' On this subject the same authority raises several other questions and gives beautiful replies.

If God illumines all souls, He must illumine all of them equally well. If each one's intelligence follows his own Karma, then no God is required. The answer is that Karma itself acts through God, though God cannot change Karma. And the analogies of the earth which yields according to the labour of the peasant, and the sun who can only ripen those fruits that are matured, are pointed out.

The theory that the soul is self-luminous or self-intelligent is refuted by the fact that the soul is only conscious when in union with the senses; and the opponent is compared to a man who would say that a man, with the full power of eye sight, finds out objects by feeling with his hands.

Man's intelligence is in fact analogous with his eyesight. He is not blind (non-intelligent) nor is his sight such as to make him see in the dark and dispense with the aid of the sun's light (God's grace).

Sivagnana Botham of Meykanda Deva

VI

SIXTH SUTRA

ON THE NATURE OF GOD AND THE WORLD.

Sutra: - That which is perceived by the senses is *Asat* (changeable.) That which is not so perceived does not exist. God is neither the one nor the other, and hence called *Siva Sat* or *Chit Sat* by the wise; *Chit* or *Siva* when not understood by the human intelligence and *Sat* when perceived with divine wisdom.

Commentary

This treats of the nature of Sat and Asat and consists of two arguments.

First Argument

Choornika: - Everything that is perceived by the human understanding is liable to decay.

Varthikam: - As an object exists or does not exist according to one or other attitude of the soul, it is established that the object perceived by the human understanding is *Asat*.

Udarana: - Hear, O! thou who art ignorant of the real nature of *Asat*. All those that are perceived by the human faculties and senses will be found to be *Asat* by him who has understood *Sat*.

O! Thou, who art not Asat. If similes are required to illustrate that the world is Asat, they are the figures formed on the water, the dreams and the cloud-car. They disappear before Him, as does darkness before the sun.

Second Argument

Choornika: - The Being so arrived at (that is not perceived by the soul) is Hara.

Varthikam: – All objects understood by us do not require a light to know them by, and all not so understood cannot be known even with a light. Hence that which is not included in these two and which is beyond the ken of human powers and is within its ken also, that is Sivam which is Sat.

Udarana: - (*a*) If the meaning of the expression that God is neither what can be proved and known by us nor what cannot be known is asked, he who has found the truth will say that He exists. He cannot be seen by the human understanding as He will then become Asat. He must be seen by the Arul Sakti of Siva who cannot be known by man. This Arul Sakti is His Foot.

Sivagnana Botham of Meykanda Deva

(*b*) The faculties by which the soul perceives are *Asat*. Therefore, none of them can perceive the One. Even thou, who so perceivest, cannot understand Him. If examined, what thou perceivest will be different from thee. He who has understood himself will perceive himself to be not different from Him, as he merges his personality in Him and understands through His *Arul*.

(*c*) If God is capable of being meditated by man, He becomes *Asat*. If He is regarded as a Being beyond human meditation, He will be a mere fiction. If He is meditated as neither, He will be a non-entity. If He is meditated as an object of meditation though He is beyond human meditation, this will be also a fiction. The *Param* can only be meditated with the aid of His *Arul*. Therefore, He is not a non-entity.

(*d*) To be known by the soul, He is not different from itself. As He is even present in its understanding it cannot know Him. As He in fact makes the soul see, its understanding cannot comprehend and point Him out to the soul, just as the eye which the soul enables it to see and yet is one with it cannot see the soul.

(*e*) God is not one who can be pointed out as "That." If so, not only will He be an object of knowledge, it will imply a *Gnatha* who understands Him as such. He is not different from the soul as an object of knowledge. He becomes one with the soul pervading its understanding altogether. The soul so feeling itself is also Sivam.

NOTES.

This Sutra contains the true and only definition of God, and all other attributes of God follow from the two given here. The way in which these attributes are derived is thus. In the first place, God must either be an object of human knowledge of He is not. If the first, everything that is perceived by us is liable to decay and change and we cannot regard God as liable to change. Therefore, God is beyond human perception and hence called Sivam or Chit (Pure Intelligence). If it is not an object of knowledge, is it nonentity? Of course, not, and hence He is 'Sat' 'that which subsists' 'The only Truth.' These two form the components of the word '*Satchithanantham*,' so freely applied to God in the Saivite and Vedantic lore. This is our only definition of God and it is seen that any definition of God must contain these elements and the conception of God could not be simplified in any degree. Stated thus, very few religionists would quarrel with our definition of God. And yet how very few of the religions of the world even those, which charges others as polytheistic and idolatrous have an ideal of God which conforms to this definition. Their traditions, beliefs and methods of worship destroy this true idea For instance if our definition of God, that He is inconceivable by the human intelligence and imperceptible to human powers, is true how are all those religions which believe in Avatars, Christianity and Vaishnavism included, reconcilable with our definition. When God is born in the flesh, is He not a tangible thing, a thing to be seen by our eye, felt by our touch and comprehended by our senses. How can we then call Him indescribable and imperceivable? How can the Author of evolution subject himself to the laws of evolution – birth and death. Is it not therefore that our sages one and all declare that – He is 'உதியா மரியா' 'இறப்பிலி பிறப்பிலி' (without birth and death). We challenge anybody to point out in the vast puranic

Sivagnana Botham of Meykanda Deva

lore, any story in which Siva is said to have been born in the flesh and the very stories which exist, only serve to illustrate the difference between Him and the so-called Immortals, namely, that Siva cannot die and be born, and that all others are capable of births and deaths, and our poet says:

"எல்லார் பிறப்பும் இறப்பும் இயற்பாவலர்தம்,
சொல்லாற் றெளிந்தேம், - நம் சோணேசர், இல்லிற்
பிறந்த கதையும் கேளேம் பேருலகில் வாழ்ந்துண்டு,
இறந்த கதையும் கேட்டிலேம்."

and every Tamil student can recall to mind the popular Stanza of Kalamegam in which he claims superiority to Vishnu who is superior to God, as Siva has no births, Vishnu's births are ten and his own are innumerable. The Choornika points out that all object and subject (mental) phenomena are liable to decay, not annihilation, but change. They so change from moment to moment, they are so evanescent that they may almost be said to have no existence at all, 'இல்லே யெனு மாயை' and these are therefore called *Asat*. And to avoid further misconception, it is defined as that which exists or does not exist according to the objective or subjective attitude of the mind, bearing in mind, however, *Asat* here includes all the phenomena of object and subject, both being objective to the soul. Asat or Maya therefore does not mean non-existent nor illusion nor Mitya. It simply means 'other than *Sat*.' And this definition has to be borne in mind fully, as the confusion of its meaning alone has given birth to the tortuosities of the Idealistic School. The latter School compares Asat to the imagined silver in the shell and the snake in a rope. That this is a false analogy, without any meaning, is easily shown. For the production of this illusory knowledge we must have previously possessed a knowledge of two realities both the shell and silver, and the snake and the rope and an imperfectly intelligent being, who by either defective vision or distance or fear &c. mistakes one thing for the other. The silver and snake, in themselves realities, are not in the shell and rope respectively but in a defective mind. In the genesis of the Asat, what supplies the places of silver, shell and defective mind must be shown. So far as the illusory knowledge of silver is concerned we have traced it to a defective mind. If myself and my human consciousness, objective and subjective is an illusion, who is the subject of this illusion. Inevitably, God. Such a God is itself illusory and He could not be self-luminous and Intelligent. The analogy gives us no sense whatever and though the objection as stated here has often and often been pressed, yet we find no book meeting it and we find the analogy repeated often enough and even by intelligent men, parrot-like. The nature of Asat is further explained in the illustration, and the similes given are in themselves real experiences while they last, and the point of comparison is simply their evanescent and temporary character.

2. The second Varthika gives one of the many dilemmas found in this work. If God is knowable by us, it will be easy enough to know Him and we do not require a superior Light to guide us to Him. If He is not knowable, then however we might try, we cannot discover Him, and the worship of God will be all vain trouble. The meaning being that it is not possible to know with what is called *Pasa* and *Pasu Gnanam i.e.*, by the human powers and by the soul itself. The Divine Light (*Pathi Gnanam*) must penetrate our soul and then we can discover Him

Sivagnana Botham of Meykanda Deva

dwelling in ourselves; and merging our personalities in Him, we become indistinguishable from Him and we can as it were, call ourselves even God, in name. At no time, can we therefore see God face to face as He, as it were, lies behind us, lives in us, part of our very being. Sivagnana Siddhi summarises the reasons thus:

"God cannot be perceived by the Human intelligence as He is not separate from the soul, as He illumines its intelligence, makes it understand whatever it thinks about, and as He has no such pride as I and mine, everything being in Him."

(*b*) and (*d*) and (*e*). Maya is object. Soul is subject. The object cannot perceive the subject; otherwise the subject will become the object and the object subject. God is true subject, and Maya and Soul are objects and hence Maya and Soul cannot perceive God. The subject receives further elaboration in the next Sutra.

(*c*) This verse discusses the various conceptions of God by the Yogis, and they are reduced to either mere idols of the human mind or fiction or nonentity, in all of which cases, the meditation of God will bring no profit whatever. When the highest conceptions of God in the Yoga philosophy are thus declared to be mere material idols or myths, it need not be pointed out that any representation of the Unknown and the Inconceivable by either the eye or the ear or any other human senses will be equally material conceptions and fruitless. This then is our real reason for the objection taken to all forms of idolatry. The religions ordinarily professing hatred of idolatry are based on such narrow philosophic foundations that they simply object to the idols of the eye – namely pictures and statues, &c., but their ordinary conceptions of God conveyed by the language and sound is equally gross and idolatrous. If you object to a male representation of God in gold or marble as your Father and 'Our Lord' and repeat other names which are mere idols of the ear, and what benefit would it bring you the worship of these mere names? If you object to locate the picture of the eye in a temple, why do you build Him a temple in words and in your mind and say 'Our Father which art in Heaven.' This heaven of your mind is as unreal a representation of God's abode as the Temple of the earth. A prayer is a mere word or sound worship, and all our mantras fall within this category. God can only be and is therefore represented by means of all the human senses, and the mental conceptions simply follow from the sensory conceptions. Of all these, however, the eye and the ear standing foremost among the most intellectual of the five gateways of knowledge, the symbolic forms of these two senses are deservedly most popular. And of these, the forms of the eye are all the varied forms of the universe, the five elements, the Sun, and the Moon, and the luminaries and all animal form chiefly man, comprised under what are called Ashta-Muhurtham; which forms are again divided into Guru, Lingam and Sangamam: Guru and Sangama comprising Living Beings and Lingam including all pictorial and sculptural representations, from the root 'lik,' meaning to write or describe. Cf. The word 'Lipika,' used in the 'Secret Doctrine.' The symbols presented to the ear, are sounds, words, names, and mantras, prayers, &c. And of all these the *Pranava* and *Sri Panchatchara* stand foremost. And these mantras form what is called *Sabda Brahm*. And how futile this worship of *Sabda Brahm* is when not accompanied by *Pathignanam* is illustrated by the Puranic story of the Rishis of the Tharukavana. Cf. the following extract from 'Barths' Religions of India. "Sacrifice is only an act of preparation, it is the best of acts but it is an act and its fruits consequently perishable. Accordingly, although whole sections of these

Sivagnana Botham of Meykanda Deva

treatises (Upanishads) are taken up exclusively with speculations on the rites, what they teach may be summed up in the words of Munduka Upanishad "Know the Atman only and away with everything else; it alone is the bridge to immortality." The Veda itself and the whole circle of sacred science are quite as sweepingly consigned to the second place. The Veda is not the true Brahm; it is only its reflection. And the science of this imperfect Brahm, this Sabda Brahm or Brahm in words is only a science of a lower order. The true science is that which has the true Brahm, The Para Brahman for its subject." That is, the Vedas themselves resolve into Asat and they cannot know Sat. These thoughts are not only found in almost every page of our sacred literature, but they can be met with even in every popular song, and story. If I attempt here any quotation, these will in themselves form matter for a separate book, but I am unwilling to leave it without a few, seeing the importance of the subject. Turning over the first few pages of 'Thiruvachakam' we meet with these:

"பரமன் காண்க"

(Behold the Supreme)

"சொற்பதங் கடந்த தொல்லோன் காண்க"

(Behold The most Ancient God who cannot be described by words)

"சித்தமுஞ்செல்லா சேடசியன் காண்க"

(Behold The Incomprehensible Being who cannot be reached by the Human mind)

"தேவரு மறியாச் சிவனே காண்க"

(Behold the Lord unknown to the Immortals)

"சொற்பதங் கடந்த தொல் லோன்
உள்ளத்துணர்ச்சியிற் கொள்ளவும் படான்
கண்முதற்புலனாற் காட்சியுமில்லோன்"

'He is passing the description of words, not comprehensible by the mind, not visible to the eye and other senses' (note here the words 'eye and other senses')

"யுரையுணர் விறந்த வொருவ போற்றி."

(Praise be to the One who is passing speech and thought)

"வேதங்கள் ஐயா வெனவோங்கி
ஆழ்ந்தகன்ற நுண்ணியனே."

(Thou hast passed far beyond the reach of the Vedas, which called loudly for Thee)

"ஓர்நாமம் ஒருருவம் ஒன்றுமில்லான்"

(He has no name, and no form and no marks whatever)

Sivagnana Botham of Meykanda Deva

"சோதிமணிமுடி சொல்லிற் சொல்லிறந்து நின்றதொன்மை
ஆதிகுணம் ஒன்றுமில்லா அந்தமிலான்."

(His Lustrous Crown is where all speech and thought cease to enter,
He has no beginning, no attributes and no end.)
Turn to the 'Thevaram.)

"அவன் அருளே கண்ணாகிக் காண்பதல்லால்.
இப்படியன் இவ்வுருவன், இவ்வண்ணத்தன்
இவனிறைவ னென்றெழுதிக் காட்டொணாதே."

(Unless you can see him with His Grace as your eye,
You cannot describe Him in words or picture, as this is the
God possessing such and such attributes, forms and qualities).

Says our Sainted Poetess Karaikal Ammayar:

"அன்றும் திருவுருவம் காணாதே யாட்பட்டேன்
இன்றும் திருவுருவம் காண்கிலேன் - என்றுந்தான்
எவ்வுருவோ நும்பிரான் என்பார்கட் கென்னுரைப்பேன்,
எவ்வுருவோ நின்னுருவம் எது."

When I first became Thy slave I did not know Thy form,
I have not seen Thy form even now.
What am I to say to those who ask me what Thy form is?
What is Thy form? Which is it? None.

Our Thayumanavar:

"உரையுணர்வு இறந்து தம்மையுணர்பவர் உணர்வி னூடே
கரையிலா இன்பவெள்ளம் காட்டிடும் முகிலே."

"சொல்லாலும் பொருளாலும் அளவையாலும்
தொடரவொண்ணா அருள்நெறி."

"குலமிலான் குணங்குறி யிலான்."

"சுருதியே சிவாகமங்களே யுங்களாற் சொல்லும்
ஒருதனிப்பொருள் அளவையீனென்னவா யுண்டோ
பொருதிரைக்கடலெண்ணினும் புகல
கருதவெட்டிடா நிறைபொருள் அளவையார் காண்பார்"

Cf. with verse (d).

Sivagnana Botham of Meykanda Deva

"அறியுந்தரமோ நானுன்னை, அறிவுக்கறிவாய் நிற்பதனால்
பிறியுந் தரமோ நீ யென்னைப் பெம்மானே - பேரின்பமதாய்
செறியும் பொருள் நீ நின்னையன்றிச் செறியாப் பொருள் நான்."

Having said so much, it might reasonably be asked, how is it, that the Saiva Religion whose Temples are more numerous than that of any other faith and are spread out from the Himalayas to Cape Comorin and the Islands beyond and from the caves of Elephanta to the Rock cut Temples of Mahabalipuram, tolerates these practices? This is the subject of the next chapter on Sadana and the reason is found there. This symbolic worship (sensory and mental) is required as Sadana for the human soul and these are not Sadhia *i.e.*, the means to attain an end, the knowledge of Sat, and not the end itself; or in the words of the extract quoted above, these are acts of preparation. The human mind, if it must progress in Spirituality, must withdraw more and more from its own self and rest itself on what it considers, the Highest, the Holiest and Loveliest and bestow upon it all its deeds, riches, and thoughts ( ). By such continued practice of Altruism and love of Sivam, who is All Love, will reach true *Bhakti* or *Pathi Gnanam*, described in the last chapter on Payan. Besides when we must worship God, we must worship in that body in which He is present, and we have before shown that the whole universe, animate and in animate, forms His body; and that all forms of nature are His. And our sages praise Him therefore:

"பெண் ஆண் அலியென்னும் பெற்றியன் போற்றி."

(Praise be to the One who is male, female, and neuter.)

"பூதங்கள்தோறு நின்றா யெனின் அல்லாற்
போக்கிலன் வரவிலன் என நினைப்புலவோர்,
கீதங்கள் பாடுதல் ஆடுதலல்லாற்
கேட்டறியோமுனைக் கண்டறிவாரை
சிந்தனைக்கும் அரியாய்."

(The sages can only sing Thy praises as the One immanent in all Nature, and withal as being the immutable and unchangeable; we have not heard of any persons who have seen Thee except in this way. Thou art beyond the reach of all thought.)

"கண்ணாலியானும் கண்டேன் காண்க."

(I have seen Thee with my eyes.)

'இன்னிசை வினையிலி சைந்தோன் காண்க.'

(Thou art present even as the Harmony in the Vina.)

"பூவினாற்றம் போன்றுயர்ந் தெங்கு மொழிவற நிறைந்து மேவிய பெருமை."

(Thy greatness in being present in one and all, like the smell in the folwer.)

Sivagnana Botham of Meykanda Deva

"அருக்கனிற் சோதி அமைத்தோன் திருத்தகு
மதியிற்றண்மை வைத்தோன் திண்டிறல்
தீயின் வெம்மை செய்தோன் பொய்தீர்
வானிற்கலப்பு வைத்தோன், மேதகு
நீரி லின்சுவை நிகழ்ந்தோன், வெளிப்பட
மண்ணிற் றிண்மைவைத்தோன், என்னென்று
எனைப் பலகோடியெனைப் பல பிறவும்
அனைத்தனைத் தவவயின் அடைத்தோன் அ:்தான்று"

(Thou art present as the Light in the sun.
Thou art present as the coolness in the moon.
Thou hast added Heat to the fire.
Thou art present even as Akas diffusing everywhere.
Thou art present even as the sweetness in water.
Thou art present even as the hardness in earth.
Thou art present in each and everything as such.
And yet art Thou not all these things.)

"பத்திவலையிற் படுவோன் காண்க."

(Thou art ensnared by Bhakti (Love).)

அருவமும் உருவமு மானாய் போற்றி.
பேராயிரமுடைய பெம்மான் போற்றி.

(Praise be to Thee who hast forms and art formless.)

(Praise be to Thee who hast thousand names.)

"கண்ணிற் காண்பதுன் காட்சி கையாற்றொழில்
பண்ணல்பூசை பகர்வது மந்திரம்.
மண்ணோ டைந்தும் வழங்குயிர் யாவுமே
யண்ணலே நின்னருள் வடிவாகும்மே."

Real seeing with our eyes is when we see Thee.
Real Pujah with our hands is when we worship Thee.
When we repeat Thy names, it is uttering manthra.
All the five elements and animate nature are Thy Gracious Forms

"வடிவெல்லாநின் வடிவென வாழ்த்திடாக்
கடியெனேனுமுன் காரணம் காண்பனோ."

(Can I hope to see Thy Truth
When I do not praise all Forms as Thy Form)

Sivagnana Botham of Meykanda Deva

"அருவெனில் உருவமுமுளை உருவெனில்
அருஉருவமு முளையவை யுபயமு மலை."

(If it is said, Thou art Formless, no, Thou hast also a Form.
If it is said, Thou hast only a form, no, Thou art also formless. Thou art neither.)

And again, when we picture in words or in our minds, God, say as the Creator, the protector and the destroyer, why should we not also picture Him to our eye as such? It is not that, when we speak of in words, God as creator &c., or think of Him as such, we have really advanced in any way in our knowledge of God. And it is, on this principle that the whole of the innumerable forms in Temple worship has grown among the Hindus. Each form and every detail in that form is symbolic of some idea or thought. These forms are such that if today all our philosophical works and Shastras, &c., are destroyed, it is possible to evolve, all our various Hindu Philosophical systems, Moral, Social and Religious from these images alone, provided we possess the key. This is not an idle boast, but it is want of space and fear of encumbering the subject with too much of my own views that forbid me to elaborate the subject further. However I will conclude this article by referring to and explaining in part the most important of the Saivite Forms, namely the image of Natesa and the Chin Mudra. It will be too great a detail if I proceed to describe the structure of the place or Temple called Chit Ambaram or Chit Akas, Chit Sabha and Pundarikapuram or the city of the Heart in the midst of which the Divine Dancer performs His Natak.

The pose is that of a dancer. And now dance is defined as the music of motion. And when, as we have shown, God manifests Himself as the great Energy or Force or Maha Chaitanyam, when He wills that the whole universe of Mind and Matter should undergo Evolution (creation, development and Reproduction). What could be more appropriate than to regard this Grand Moving Force as a great Dancer. In the words of our sage –

'காட்ட வனல் போல் உடல் கலந்துயிரையெல்லாம்,
ஆட்டுவிக்கும் நட்டுவன் எம்மண்ணணலென வெண்ணாய்.'

(Our God is the Dancer who like the heat latent in the firewood diffuses His Power in Mind and Matter and Makes them dance in their turn.) I prefer again to quote the famous author of 'Chidambara Mummanikkovai' in order to explain a few of the other Symbols.

'பூமலி கற்பகப் பூத்தேள் வைப்பு
நாமநீர் வரைப்பின் நானில வளாகமும்
ஏனைய புவனமும் எண்ணீங்குயிரும்
தானே வகுத்ததுன் தமருகக் கரமே
தனித்தனி வகுத்த சராசரப்பகுதி
யனைத்தையும் காப்பதுன் அமைத்த கைத்தலமே
தோற்றுபு நின்ற அத் தொல்லுலகடங்கலும்
ஆற்றுவது ஆரழல் அமைத்ததோர் கரமே
ஈட்டிய வினைப்பயன் எவற்றையும் மறைத்துநின்

Sivagnana Botham of Meykanda Deva

றாட்டுவ தாகும்நின் ஊன்றியபதமே;
அடுத்த இன்னுயிர்கட்கு அளவில் பேரின்பம்
கொடுப்பது முதல்வநின் குஞ்சித பதமே
இத்தொழில் ஐந்தும்நின் மெய்த்தொழில்.'

Roughly translated, the passage means 'O my Lord, Thy Hand holding the sacred drum (Damaruka - உடுக்கை) has made and arranged the Heavens and the Earth and other worlds and innumerable souls. Thy raised Hand protects the *Chethana* and *Achethana Prapancha* which Thou hadst created. All these worlds are changed by Thy Hand bearing Fire. Thy Sacred Foot, planted on the ground, furnishes rest to the tired soul struggling in the toils of Karma and eating the fruits thereof. It is Thy lifted Foot which grants eternal bliss to those who approach Thee. These *Pancha Krithya* are in fact Thy true Handy-work.

The curious may enquire how the hand with the drum signifies creation or creative Power. Those who have read Mrs. Annie Beasant's Lecture on Sound will have noted that when creation is started Sound or Natham is the first product, out of which all other tatwas are evolved, and the Damarukam is probably the oldest and most primitive sound producing instruments known to the Aryans and which, the use of it still in all religious observances also points to.

The *Chin Mudra* found in the Person of the Divine Guru *Dakshina Murthi* explains the nature of the three *padarthas* and the difference of the *Banda* and *Moksha* conditions. For a fuller account of this symbol, see the pages of 'The Theosophist.'

Sivagnana Botham of Meykanda Deva

CHAPTER - III. SPECIAL: SATHANAVIAL

VII - SEVENTH SUTRA

RESPECTING THE SOUL

Sutra: - In the presence of Sat, everything else (cosmos-Asat) is *Sunyam* (is non-apparent) Hence Sat cannot perceive *Asat*. As Asat does not exist, it cannot perceive Sat. That which perceives both cannot be either of them. This is the Soul (called *Sadasat*).

Note. This treats of the nature of the Soul and consists of three arguments.

First Argument

Choornika: - *Hara* has no experience of *Pasa*.

Varthikam: - As, before the Perfect and Eternal Intelligence, the imperfect and acquired intelligence (falsehood) is shorn of its light, it is therefore established that in the presence of *Siva Sat*, *Asat* loses its light.

Udarana: - Hara who is not separate (from *Pasu* and *Pasa*) cannot know them as objects. So, He cannot know *Asat* as different even when He knows it. Evil Asat ceases to exist before Him, as does darkness before the Sun.

Second Argument

Choornika: - *Pasa* cannot know *Hara*.

Varthikam: - *Asat* is non – intelligent as it will be found to be so when examined closely.

Udarana: - The ignorant man who follows a mirage as water, will find it to be false when he reaches it. So, the soul whom God's grace has not reached will find Asat to be Sat. As Asat does not exist, it cannot know (*Sat*). Therefore, learn that *Asat* has no understanding.

Third Argument

Choornika: - The soul lives in both.

Varthikam: - It is established that the soul which has such double perception is neither of them; as the soul is that which perceives both, understands on being taught, and exists in either condition eternally.

Udarana: -O! Thou who art engaged in deep studies. The soul has knowledge of both Sat and Asat and hence is neither of them. It does not appear as equivalent to either of them, nor is it nonentity being neither of them. Its nature is like the smell of the flower which at one time was non-apparent, though existing in the plant and at another time became apparently visible.

Sivagnana Botham of Meykanda Deva

(2) Thou art not *Sat*, as thy understanding is changeful and imperfect, becoming deranged in disease and recovering its brightness when medicines are administered. Thou art neither *Asat* as thou hast to eat the fruits of *Karma*, knowingly performed by thyself, and which *Asat* cannot know and enjoy.

(3) Ignorance (Agnanam) will not arise from God who is the true intelligence as it is Asat (like darkness before light). The soul which is ever united to God is co-eternal with Him. The connection of ignorance with the soul is like the connection of Salt with the water of the sea.

NOTES

We have proved to ourselves the existence of the three categories or Padarthas, Pathi, Pasu, and Pasa in the first chapter. We have learned to distinguish them further in the second chapter. And now what is the use of all this knowledge? All knowledge and all philosophy will be utterly useless if it will not lead us to believe that we have a better end to attain to and to action that will bring about this end. The true end or Siddhantha is what is treated off in Chapter IV and this chapter preceding it is appropriately devoted to the treatment of the action or Sadana or means of attaining the True End. Now in proceeding to begin Sadana, if we begin as the author of *Vichara Sagar* begins, 'I am God, I worship myself. Why should I worship any other?' we cannot achieve much. Unless we can distinguish ourselves from God, we cannot attempt to become God. This Sutra therefore enjoins on the person beginning his practice a further caution not to mistake himself for God, thereby distinguishing between Sat, Asat and Satasat and showing also what becomes of the lower planes when we pass on to the Higher. Asat has already been explained to mean other than Sat. This word and Sunyam do not mean non-existent and nonentity but also mean non-apparent or non-luminous or non-distinguishable (விளங்காமை, பிரகாசியாமை). The Ganges pouring from its thousand mouths into the broad sea preserves its taste and reddish colour for miles and miles beyond, but as we proceed down, the water gradually loses its taste and colour and finally, sure as anything, we cannot find it. It is lost completely. No, it is not lost. The great sea which is greater than the great Gauges has completely engulfed and covered it up and in consequence it is the sea and its Salt and not the Ganges and its taste that is apparent to us. Sea is Sat and the Ganges mingling with it is Asat or Sunyam. Again, darkness is as real an experience of our sight as day light. We speak of darkness engulfing the whole world at night; but with the first streak of dawn, darkness has completely fled and vanished. Has it? And if so, where to? No, it has neither gone not fled anywhere nor has it become non-existent. Darkness is present in Light and is completely absorbed in it. The greater Glory and Power of the one subjugates or covers the power of the other.

We have elsewhere referred to the analogy of the sunlight and stars. The author of Sivagnana Siddhi calls this 'முனைத்திடாமை' which is explained to mean, that God cannot distinguish it as apart from Him as we distinguish one object from another. Knowledge and consciousness is only relative; and in the Presence of the Absolute, the All, there could be no relativity and no knowledge or consciousness. Hence Sat cannot perceive Asat. As elsewhere

Sivagnana Botham of Meykanda Deva

explained, in the subjective state, the object vanishes. That is in pure subjective consciousness, object consciousness merges, becomes indistinguishable, there is no knowledge of object.

2. *Asat* cannot perceive Sat as it cannot rise above itself in perception and as it is itself the object of the soul. So it is doubly distant from Sat.

3. This argument brings out the whole subject of *Atma Darsan* and shows how the soul can be seen or perceived. The soul cannot be perceived directly as this is physically and psychologically impossible. It is by learning to distinguish itself from other things that it can know what it really is. There are two such things from which it has to distinguish itself, namely, Sat and Asat. In the human condition, it is one with *Asat* and the first step in spiritual progress is to distinguish itself and then slowly to separate itself from Asat. But it should not be supposed from the fact of the soul rising to its own plane from Asat that it is a compound or an effect or Asat itself. The soul did exist in Asat even previously though in a latent or unperceived condition and it rises out of Asat as the smell of the flower rises out of the tree or plant in which it was not perceived before. Rising to itself, the soul should not stop there, but must again learn to distinguish itself from Sat and then try its best to lift itself into the plane of Sat, with which also it was connected as the flower and the plant. "சீவனுக்குள்ளே சிவமணம் பூத்தது" (In the tree of Life (soul) the sweet blossom of Sivam blossoms out). In the banda condition, the soul appeared only as Asat, and when the banda is removed, freedom is obtained and it then appears not itself but as Sivam. So, in neither condition, its own nature is subordinated to the one to which it is connected for the time being, and apart from either, it cannot find a resting place and it lives therefore in both.

Though at all times all the three existed together, yet at one time, Soul and Sat were non-apparent and Asat alone apparent like the tree before blossoming; and at another time, Asat disappears and soul is enveloped in Sivam and the brightness and sweetness of the flower alone shines out.

Cf. 'Thirumanthiram.'

"அனாதி சிவரூபமாகிய ஆன்மா
தனாதிமலத்தாற் நடைப்பட்டு நின்றது
தனாதிமலமும் தடையற்றபோதே
யனாதிசிவ ரூபமாகிய வாறே."

(The soul which in its real condition is of the form of Sivam is confined and conditioned by its connection with Malam; when this bantham therefore ceases, it assumes the form of Sivam).

(*c*) The last illustration contains a favorite analogy. God is the sea or the vast space giving room to a vast volume of water and things contained in it, "the all Container" "The *Sarva Viyapaka*." The water is the soul which is *Vyapti* and the salt of the water is the *Malam* which is *Vyappia*. The import of the analogy in this place is that though it is the sea which gives room to the water and the salt, yet the salt does not attach itself to the sea (space) but to the water. And the salt though it is always present in sea water, the water in its original or real condition, is not so connected and this connection can be separated.

Sivagnana Botham of Meykanda Deva

VIII - EIGHTH SUTRA

THE WAY IN WHICH SOULS OBTAIN WISDOM

Sutra: - The Lord appearing as *Guru* to the Soul which had advanced in *Tapas* (Virtue and Knowledge) instructs him that he has wasted himself by living among the savages of the five senses; and on this, the soul, understanding its real nature leaves its former associates, and not being different from Him, becomes united to His Feet.

Commentary

This explains the Path of attaining Gnanam, and consists of four arguments.

First Argument

Choornika: - Souls will obtain wisdom from *Tapas*.

Varthikam: – *Moksha* cannot be obtained when performing *Sariya, Kriya,* and *Yoga,* unless the supreme *Gnanam* is attained by *Tapas* effected in all previous births.

Udarana: - (*a*) Those who have performed *Tapas* enjoy its fruits in the various *Tapalokas* (Heavens). And then they attain good births, so that they may get rid of even these desires, by eating the fruits of these desires, and attain *Gnanam*. This is what the learned in the *Shastras* say.

(*b*) The bliss secured by the much-praised sacrificial acts will be like the pleasure derived by the hungry man after eating and who again becomes hungry. The soul will join its *Gnana Guru* when by its indestructible *Tapas* (*Sariya, Kriya* and *Yoga*) its good and bad *Karma* become perfectly balanced.

Second Argument

Choornika: - He who comes as the *Sarguru* of the souls is *Hara*.

Varthikam: - It is established that the Lord appearing as *Guru* will teach the souls, as not being separate from the souls, He shines in the light of the souls as His body.

Udarana: - (*a*) God imparts *Gnanam* to *Vignanakalars* as they dwell in Himself; to *Pralayakalars*, He appears as *Guru* in His divine form and imparts *Gnanam*; and to *Sakalars*, He appears as *Guru* concealing himself in human form and imparts *Gnanam*.

(*b*) The souls will not attain *Gnanam* unless imparted by God in order. Those (Pralayakalar and Sakalar) who are instructed by the Perfect Lord of the world, receive such instructions in the 2nd and 3rd persons respectively. Those (Vignana Kalar) who do not receive such imperfect instruction, attain *Moksha Gnanam* from God by intuition.

(*c*) The milk and tears, which did not exist before, appear in the person of the well-adorned mother after the birth of the child as the result of her love. Who will therefore understand the Lord who is present in the soul, unperceived, like the *Akas* in the water, if he did not appear in the form of the Divine *Guru*?

Third Argument

Choornika: - The soul does not see itself when in union with the five senses.

Varthikam: - The souls, being blinded by the senses forget their real nature, as the senses do not show the soul its own nature but only put before it, its own impressions, just like the colors reflected on a mirror.

Udarana: - The soul, who, after reflection that the knowledge derived from the material senses is only material, like the colors reflected on a mirror, and that these color-like sensations are different from itself, and after perceiving such false knowledge as false, understands the Truth, will become the servant of God who is different from such *Asat*.

Fourth Argument

Choornika: - The soul will know itself when it forgets the senses.

Varthikam: - The soul reaches the feet of its Lord when it sees itself to be different from the senses, just as a man reaches the ground, when the rope of the swing breaks.

Udarana: - (*a*) The soul which becomes bound with Pasam, like the river flood when stopped by an embankment, will not leave the Divine Feet of the Lord, who is unchangeable, after once attaining Them, on being freed from the ties of the world, like the flood which reaches the sea on the embankments being destroyed.

(*b*) If every object is God, then no body need attain God's feet. If He is not everything, If He is not God. Everything cannot see Him, as though the eye sees all objects, all the other senses cannot see. Understand the supremacy of eye-sight in persons who recover their eye-sight.

(*c*) O Thou, who hast found that thou art not the five senses! The *Sakala* who has reached the Divine *Guru*, after leaving the knowledge of the five senses, yet is not separated from the five senses. If the result of Mala and Karma again surround him, as the separated moss covers the water again, a little while after a stone is thrown, let him remove it by contemplating on Him who is never separate from him.

Sivagnana Botham of Meykanda Deva

NOTES

After showing, in the last *Sutra*, what the Soul has to achieve, this Sutra proceeds to explain the Sadanas and the fruits of such *Sadana*.

To begin with, the soul, by its practice of *Tapas* in all its past and present birth must have acquired sufficient knowledge and spirituality as to be able to attain *Gnanam*. *Tapas* as here used means and includes three out of the four *Pathams* or Paths described in this school namely *Sariya*, *Kriya*, and *Yoga*. *Sariya* and *Kriya* include all kinds of altruistic and Moral and Religious practices. All these three which are placed in an ascending order bring about what is called 'இருவினையொப்பு and மலபரிபாகம்' (balancing of the good and bad *Karma*, and the maturing of *Mala* before it can be dropped). The practice of these *Sadanas* develop in the soul, true knowledge (*Gnanam*) and Love (*Bakhti*) and God who is all Love, appears as *Guru* and imparts *Gnanam*, the fourth *Patham* by showing it its true nature; and the Soul attaining Gnanam frees itself from Asat and reaches the Feet of the Sat. Hence the four paths, Sariya, Kriya, Yoga and Gnanam lead to four fruits or Sadhia, namely '*Iruvinai Oppu*' '*Malaparipaga*' '*Sargurudarsana*' and '*Sattinipada*' (reaching Divine Grace). The illustrations to the first argument point out that it is possible to attain a good many powers and enjoyments by the practice of *Tapas*; none of which however will be lasting or lead one to freedom and eternal bliss. They only beget further Karma and further births. The true *Tapasi* will aim at destroying all Karma and reach his true *Guru*. And the second argument points out who the Sarguru is and illustration (c) shows how He is to be obtained. This Guru cannot be any other than God and except by His touch, it is impossible to obtain *Gnanam*. By practice of True *Tapas*, by intense devotion and Love, it is easy to attract God to one-self as his Guru.

"அன்பு சிவமும் மிரண்டென்பா றறிவிலார்
அன்பே சிவமாவ தாரு மறிந்திலார்
அன்பே சிவமாக தாரு மறிந்தபின்
அன்பே சிவமா யமர்ந்திருப்பாரே."

"The ignorant think that God and Love are different.
None knows that God and Love are the same.
Did all men know that God and Love are the same.
They would repose in God as Love."
                                       (Thirumanthiram)

It will therefore be seen that the whole of the moral, Religious and psychical (Yoga) practices are simply preparatory acts and can never be ends in themselves and can never be of any use, unless the true end is kept in view.

As our Thayumanavar says:

"விரும்பும் சரியைமுதல் மெய்ஞ்ஞான நான்கும்
அரும்புமலர் காய்கனிபோ லன்றோ பராபரமே."

Sivagnana Botham of Meykanda Deva

(O My Lord, are not the four Paths from the much desired *Sariya* to the *Gnanam* like the unopened flower, the blossom, the unripe fruit and the ripe fruit). And the author of Ozhivilodukkam who is a true Siddhantin appropriately devotes three of his chapters to *Sariya Kalatri, Kriya Kalatri*, and *Yoga Kalatri*, in which he exposes and reviles in unmeasured terms the practices of impostors, false prophets and Pharisees.

And again, the doctrine of the Divine Guru as expounded here should be particularly noted and distinguished. In fact, if one takes all the beliefs and practices of every religion and every faith all the world over, it is just possible to reduce them all to one common law and common principle. Through sheer forget fullness of this common principle and through distance of time and place, the true belief and practice has been lost sight of; and if preserved, the mere shadow of them are preserved; and when people speculate on them fresh, all sorts of theories and explanations are given. And these remarks apply with very great force to the doctrine in question. So far is true, that unless God comes down as Man and Guru and touches man with His *Arul* or Grace, he cannot attain salvation. But when we proceed further and ask who this Guru is, when and how he appears and acts, why and wherefore he appears, whom he purifies, and how he purifies, and how he purifies, the answers are returned as each man's fancy dictates to him, without any reference to God's and Nature's laws. The doctrine of atonement is as puerile as the belief of the villager who seeks to appease his village deity by sacrificing a cock or hen; and the doctrine of mediation, admittedly based on no higher principle than that of human agency, instances of which are the Judge, prisoner and lawyer, King, subjects, and Viceroy, &c., which clearly involves the impairing of the Omniscience and Omni potency of the Supreme Ruler of the universe, is equally unsatisfactory. If the Guru is Himself God, how could he be a mediator. God is in man and can appear to him as man but cannot become man. He dwelleth in our hearts and understands all our wants and He meets all our wants. He knows our disease and our sufferings and He has a balm already prepared for us. Nobody need therefore tell Him, what we want, what our disease and pain are and to crave His mercy for us, as He is all Love and All mercy. There is no mediation. The touch of the Guru converts the already prepared baser metal into Gold. His touch is as the surgeon's lancet which opens out and heals an abscess fully matured. Just as the loving mother runs and takes to her breast the crying child, so God reaches us the instant we lift our voice to Him. It is also seen that it is necessary for God to appear as Man, only so far, man and Sakalars are concerned; and that as far as other advanced souls, *Vignana Kalars* are concerned, He induced Gnanam in them intuitively. The necessity so far as man is concerned arises, because man cannot know otherwise.

Again, the sinner to expect salvation, as he lisps, while he dies some dead names and words is absurd, as also to expect that some dead names will produce such effects for all time to come. Tested by the truth as laid down in this Sutra, the ordinary observances and beliefs of almost every religions, Saiva and other Hindu Religions included, will be a mere mockery and sham; but still it will be observed, that even among Hindu Religions, the Saiva Religion does not tolerate hierarchy in any form.

3. The human soul is compared to the son of a king stolen by savages, at his very birth and living among them and who can never understand his identity until informed recognized,

Sivagnana Botham of Meykanda Deva

by the King himself. The soul, in its nature, of pristine purity, develops itself only, as its cosmic covering also evolves, and will recover itself only with the touch of the Divine Guru. The soul is again compared to a painted glass or mirror in which the identity of the mirror is lost and will not be recovered unless the paint is washed away.

4. The language 'Reaching the Feet of the Lord' is significant. The freed soul does not become co-extensive (if we can use the word) with God. It simply becomes imbedded in it, a mere drop in the vast ocean, a mere trace as it were. Even among Saivas, not to say of other schools among Hindu Philosophers, even among the commentators of this very book, there are differences of opinion as regards the condition of the freed soul in union with God. The opinion of the author may be however taken as stated above. The soul is like the flickering lamp tossed by the wind and darkness and which loses itself completely in bright noon-day-light and remains still and quiet.

There is eternal joy however in such a change and passage, and it may be compared to the great joy of the person passing from darkness to light and of the blind person recovering his eyesight.

(c) This illustration points out that the bodily infirmities or the effects do not cease altogether even after the touch of the Divine Guru. These infirmities have been so firmly rooted in man and had become so strong that it takes even sometime after *Sarguru Darsan* to remove the effects of its former association completely During this interval, the soul becoming freed is enjoined to contemplate God, and this last injunction is what is elaborated in the next *Sutra*.

Sivagnana Botham of Meykanda Deva

IX - NINTH SUTRA

ON THE PURIFICATION OF THE SOUL

Sutra: - The soul, on perceiving in itself with the eye of Gnanam, the Lord who cannot be perceived by the human intellect or senses, and on giving up the world (Pasa) by knowing it to be false as a mirage, will find its rest in the Lord. Let the soul contemplate *Sri Panchatchara* according to Law.

Commentary

This treats of the manner of purifying the soul and consists of three arguments.

First Argument

Choornika: - The soul can perceive *Hara* only with His *Gnanam*.

Varthikam: - That the soul should see the Lord by its eye of Gnanam, is established by the fact that the Lord cannot be perceived by the human senses and faculties and is otherwise perceivable.

Udarana: - (*a*) A person after examining the nerves, bones, pus, phlegm of which he is composed of and not finding, what he is, arrives at the knowledge that he must understand with some other intelligence; and unless he then understands his God and his own self with the aid of *Hara*, how else is he to understand his own self?

(*b*) The eye, which points out all things, cannot see itself nor can it see the soul which enables it to see. And the soul, which enables the eye to see, cannot see itself nor God who enables it to see. As God is one with the soul when it so understands, so examine the way in which he so exist in thy understanding.

Second Argument

Choornika: - *Hara* will appear to the soul when it relinquishes the world (Pasa.)

Varthikam: - It should be found by experience when the soul sees the world which is *Asat* as *Asat*, it will find its being, where it was, before in *Gnana Sorupam*; just as when the colors reflected on a mirror are understood to be colors, we can see the mirror itself.

Udarana: - (*a*) Will not the Lord who is *Nirguna, Nirmala*, eternal Happiness, *Tatparam* (above all things) and beyond comparison, and appears to the soul when it gets rid of the *Tatwas* such as *Akas*, &c., will not He appear as a far transcending Wonder and as an inseparable Light of its understanding?

(*b*) When thou seest all the world as *Asat*, then understand what remains is clearly *Sat*. Yet thou who hither to hadst knowledge of the world art not *Sat*. If thou unitest thyself to *Sat* and obtainest its Divine Form, *Asat* will altogether leave thee.

Sivagnana Botham of Meykanda Deva

(c) When the soul leaves *Asat* on finding that what he had known is not Sat, and examines the Lord of the universe in itself and perceives Him as itself, it leaves its *Pasam* by His aid, as the snake bitten man is cured by the Snake charmer contemplating on *Garuda*.

Third Argument

Choornika: - If the soul contemplates Sri Panchatchara its *Vasana Mala* will disappear.

Varthikam: - Understand that the contemplation of *Sri Panchatchara* according to Law is herein enjoined for the purpose of freeing the soul of its hankering after evil, which it does by its long association, even after attaining the knowledge of the *Gneya*, just like the worm feeding on the bitter margosa bark returns to it even after tasting the sweets of the sugar cane.

Udarana: - (a) If the soul perceives by pronouncing *Sri Panchatchara* that it is the servant of *Hara* and does puja to Him in the region of the heart by means of *Sri Panchatchara* and performs *Homam* by the same means in the region of *Kundalini* (navel) and contemplates Him between the eyebrows, the Lord will appear to the soul and the soul will become His servant.

(b) If the soul sees the Lord in his heart as the shadow Planets *Ragu* and *Kethu* are seen in the Sun and in the Moon, the Lord will appear as the Light of the soul, just as the latent fire appears when pieces of wood are rubbed together. The soul will then become His servant, just as the iron becomes fire when heated. Therefore, contemplate on Sri Panchatchara.

(c) If the real nature of the Heart of the Lotus is examined its stalk will be the 24 *Tatwas* beginning with earth; its petals will be *Vidya Tatwas* and *Sutta Vidya*; its pollen the 64 Kalas of *Iswara* and *Sathasiva*; its ovary *Sakti*, the essence of the *Kalas*; and the seeds the 51 forms *Natham*; and the *Arul Sakti* of the Lord Siva rests on it. Therefore, contemplate on *Sri Panchatchara*.

NOTES

This Sutra treats of the Sadana that is required for the *Gnana padha*, and during the period after *Sarguru Darshan*, and before becoming *Jivan Mukta*, and while in the human body. The necessity for any *Sadana* at all during this period is because as is indicated in the 3rd argument, the human soul by its long association with *Asat*, sometimes forgets itself even after it has found out its own nature and though it cannot do evil, there is a hankering after evil. This is what is called *Vasana Malam* or *Thosham*, evil of habit or association. The man whose sight is restored in the beginning loves to shut his eyes a little. The worm even tasting sweetness forgets it and delights to eat the bitter bark by its long habit previously contracted. The reason why it lingers is shown further on by the illustrations of the potter's wheel which revolves even after the potter's hand is withdrawn, and the empty asafoetida pot. The *Sadana* given in this *Sutra* for removing this *Vasana Malam* is the contemplation of *Sri Panchatchara* or say *Pranavam*, and here we pass into the subject of *Aha Dyanam* as distinguished from *Pura Dyanam*, esoteric worship from exoteric worship. There is, however, a correspondence

Sivagnana Botham of Meykanda Deva

between these two and the correspondence is that between a reality and a Symbol. The various rituals employed in Temple worship correspond to various real spiritual practices employed in esoteric worship. The subject is too abstruse even for me, especially as I am not yet an initiate, and any elaboration of it is altogether beyond the scope of this work. The object of the original work itself is to lay down and explain the foundations, the basic principles of our Philosophy and Religion and I need not pass beyond this either. The principle of this *Sadana* is contained in the 2nd argument and brought out more fully in illustration (c). This principle is what is called *Sohambavana*. *Soham* is from the root 'Sa' meaning It (denoting Brahm) and Aham meaning I or Me (denoting soul). The word 'Sivoham' is also its equivalent; and the word means Brahm is myself or I and Brahm. This in fact is also the purport of the four Maha Vakyas in the Veda which are 4 Mantras intended for practice or *Sadana* and to be taught by the *Guru* to the initiate. Like every other *Sadana* provided for the first three stages which are mistaken for the end itself by Vedantists and these proclaim that they are themselves God. And the caution is therefore conveyed and repeated several times in the 1st and 2nd arguments and in the illustrations (see especially illustration 2 (*b*)) that the soul practicing *Sohambavana* should not mistake itself for God. This practice of the *Gnani* therefore is as much a symbolic worship or *Bavana* as that of the Yogi (illustration 2 (c) Sutra VI.) But the *Yogi* gains certain *Sadhia* or *Siddhis* by his *Bavana* and the *Gnani* also gains something and what this is shown in the 3rd argument. The great mistake of Vedantic writers and Vedantic books consists in this that instead of treating of the Maha Vakya in its proper place and confining it within its proper scope, they discuss it, when they speak of proof or in the argumentative or expository stage. And this is what makes many of these books ridiculous. To say to ordinary mortals that he is God and he must believe himself to be God is certainly absurd when as we have seen above, to whom and by whom this instruction (Mantra) has to be imparted and even then, accompanied with proper caution. This then is what constitutes throwing pearls before swine and who is the more blame-worthy of the two?

I must now proceed to explain the principle of *Sohambavana* contained in 2 (*c*). As the illustration of the Snake charmer points out, this is the under lying principle of all Mantras. By frequent practice of the Mantra, by contemplation of the principle underlying the Mantra, the person contemplating becomes converted into the Mantric idea or principle itself, *i.e.*, the idea becomes the actuality and this also explains the Siddhis acquired by Yogis by Will-power. So, when the Gnani contemplates on *Sri Panchatchara* and that he is Brahm or Sivam, he becomes Brahm itself. Here note again the difference. It is not total conversion. What happens is this. What was before non-apparent and in himself becomes apparent as the invisible shadow planets become visible in the Sun and Moon at Eclipse time. With this effect, again, however, that the first (soul) goes down and becomes non-apparent and the other (Brahm) becomes apparent and Supreme, as the invisible oxygen always in contact with a piece of wood, when it chemically combines with the wood, altogether changes its form into its own as a living, shining fire (3rd argument illustration b). Here it is seen, it is the fire or oxygen (Brahm) that it is supreme, and not a piece of wood or iron (soul) which the former subordinates. So even in Mukti, the soul is really the servant of God.

Sivagnana Botham of Meykanda Deva

CHAPTER IV. PAYANIAL
X - TENTH SUTRA
THE WAY OF DESTROYING PASA

Sutra: - As the Lord becomes one with the Soul in its human condition, so let the Soul become one with Him and perceive all its actions to be His. Then will it lose all its *Mala*, *Maya*, and *Karma*.

Commentary

This Sutra treats of the way of destroying *Pasa*, and consists of two arguments.

First Argument

Choornika: - Become one with Hara.

Varthikam: - It is pointed out, here, that the Soul should become one with Parameshwara as He had become one with it, as, when it does so, it joins His feet by losing its pride of self and self-knowledge.

Udarana: - When the Soul asserts its own knowledge by distinguishing its acts from those of others, the Lord losing His identity, will appear as the Soul. But the Soul which says that there is no such thing as itself and that all actions are His, the Lord unites to His feet and reveals His real self to it.

Second Argument

Choornika: - Consider all your actions to be those of the Lord.

Varthikam: - It is enjoined that the Soul should perceive its actions to be those of the Lord's unceasingly, as it will not act, except with His *Arul*, and, in consequence, ignorance and Karma will not enter it.

Udarana: - (a) If the soul determines that the senses are not itself, and that their actions are not its own, and that the perceived objects are also not itself, and that it is the servant of Hara, and then arrives at the conclusion, that everything is His work, then none of the actions of the Soul which, thus, attributes every work to Him, will affect it, in whatever body it may be encased. And *Praraptha Karma* will also then cease.

(b) As it is the prerogative of the great to protect those who resort to them, so God raises those who approach Him and yet bears no ill-will (to the rest). He transforms His devotees into His own Form; and the rest who do not approach Him, He makes them eat the fruits of their own *Karma*. These two functions He performs according to the deserts of each.

Sivagnana Botham of Meykanda Deva

(*c*) Like the smell which is present in the pot, even after the asafoetida is removed, the effects of the *Gnani's* previous *Karma* will be felt in the material body and yet they will not furnish food for a future birth, as it, having been transformed into the Lord is fixed in Him.

(*d*) Like the *Siddha* who, sitting in fire, is not burnt by it, and like the horseman who, riding on the fleetest animal, does not lose his hold, the *Gnanis* who, ascertaining the true path, fix their thoughts on the Divine Feet of *Hara*, will not, though, having perception through the senses, be affected by such perception, and leave their true nature.

(*e*) If one, finding the truth that he is *Sadasat*, understands only with *Sivagnanam*, he will not be affected by *Anavamala* and will become united to *Sat*. Then will not the affections of the senses influence him, just as the darkness will have no effect before the fierce light of the Sun.

NOTES

In the last Sutra, it was enjoined that the soul should contemplate on *Sri Panchatchara* for the purpose of effecting its purification. The present chapter treats of the *Palan* or ends to be achieved by the *Sadanas* mentioned in the foregoing chapter. The end, it is agreed on all sides, is what is called *Moksha* or *Mukti* or "*Veedu*" in Tamil. The word literally means freed or freedom and it therefore imports two things. When the soul attains *Mukti* it is freed from ignorance or *Pasam* (*Pasa* and *Pasu Gnanam*) and attains *Pathi Gnanam*. The very act which separates the soul from *Pasam* (*Jagat*) unites it to the *Pathi* (*Brahm*) as was before illustrated by the case of the man reaching the ground by the breaking of the rope of the swing. Of these two results of *Mukti*, this *Sutra* treats of *Pasatchaya* or the mode by which the soul is freed of *Pasa*. This is achieved by the soul becoming one with God and by considering all its actions as those of the Lord. Becoming one with God means attaining Adwaitha relation is, the Sutra points out that the soul should become one with God in *Mukti* as God was one with the soul in its *bantha* condition. This relationship is further explained in the next Sutra in explaining the attainment of *Pathi Gnanam*. Some of the *Purvapaksha* theories relating to the condition of the soul in Mukti are as follows: -

Freedom or unity is reached,

1. When the *Akas* of the pot unites with the outer *Akas* by the breaking of the pot;

2. When the man mistaken for a post is ascertained to be a man;

3. When the cause of the earthen pot is found to be earth (causation);

4. When the colour or quality of a thing is found to be united to the thing itself, (a thing and its inseparable attribute);

5. When the iron becomes red hot, (iron and heat);

6. When water is mixed with the milk;

7. When the charmer becomes one with the object of his Mantra;

Sivagnana Botham of Meykanda Deva

8. When the heated iron absorbs water;

9. When the man becomes one with the devil when possessed;

10. When the fire-wood is covered up by the flames;

11. When the lamp is lighted before the midday sun;

12. When two lovers become one by the result of their love;

13. When two friends become united by friendship;

14. When two animals are one by mere resemblance or similarity such as colour, &c.

It would be noticed that some of these relationships are exactly what have been already used as illustration in the preceding pages, but it should be carefully noted that they are used as mere illustrations only and nothing more. These are not to be mistaken for the actual truth itself and the only similarity in nature which approximates almost to truth itself is found in the relation of the soul and God in the *bantha* condition. In the *bantha* condition soul exists and God is non-existent; in Mukti, God exists and Soul is non-existent; yet in either case neither God nor Soul is non-existent.

The relationship contemplated in the last Sutra is what is called that of *Gnathuru*, *Gnana* and *Gneya*. Mukti cannot be attained if this relation is preserved and unless Adwaitha relation is established. It is not even sufficient if it becomes one, for the purpose of rooting out all Karma; and the soul is therefore enjoined to consider its actions as those of the Lord. These injunctions are of course for the *Gnani* attaining Mukti even in this life. So long as the human body lasts, the effects of *Praraptha* will sometimes linger as the smell of the asafoetida lingers in the pot, or as the author of *Sivagnana Siddhi* adds, the wheel of the pot continues to resolve for sometime even after the hand of the potter is removed. *Sanjitha Karma* is destroyed by the very touch of the *Gnana Guru* as the seed coming in contact with fire. Praraptha continues and it is destroyed by practicing the Sadana contained in the last Sutra; and its effects or Vasana are destroyed by the condition attained by the *Jivan Mukta*. But so long as the human body continues, some acts will have to be performed by the *Jivan Mukta*, and it is shown by the illustrations, these acts will not produce any other acts or form the seed for any future *Karma* or *Akamia* and no other births will be induced.

The arguments point out why the condition attained by the *Jivan Mukta* has the effect of destroying *Pasa*. It is because the soul thereby loses its *Ahankara* and *Mamakara* or *Anava* and this last is the source of all evil, all Karma and successive births.

The learned commentator of *Ozhivilodukkum* and the author of several excellent devotional works argues out the existence of the three *Padarthas* and the rest of the doctrine from the word *Mukti* or *Veedu* itself, in the following stanza: -

வீடென் றறைதரு சொற்குப் பொருளோ விடுதலை யாதலினால்;
வீக்குண் டோனும் கட்டுண் டோனும் விளங்கும் திடமாக,

Sivagnana Botham of Meykanda Deva

பீடு கட்டுத் தானாய் விட்டுப் பெயராது இது சடமாம்,
பிணி பட்டோன் அசுதந்தரனாகும் பிணிபெயரச் செய்வோன்
நீடு சுதந்தர முண்டா மொருவன் எனுமிவ் வேதுவினால்,
நிகழ்பதி பசுபாசம் மென முப்பொருள் நிச்சய மென்றருளி,
வேடனை வெல்லும் குருவா யெனையாள் மெய்ப்பொருள் நீயன்றோ,
வேதகிரிப்பவ ரோக வயித்திய வேணி முடிக்கனியே.
- Chidambara Swamigal of Tiruporur.

"As the word *Mukti* or *Veedu* means freedom, it imports clearly a Free Being and an unfreed or fettered being. The fetters can never become removed of themselves. Hence this *Bantham* is *Jatam* or *Asat*. So saying, O Thou Healer of Sins! Thou hast appeared to me as my Sar Guru, the victor of the savages (of the senses) and hast taught me to infer for certain the three *Padarthas*, *Pathi*, *Pasu* and *Pasa* from the word *Mukti* and hast graciously taken me as thy servant.

Sivagnana Botham of Meykanda Deva

XI - ELEVENTH SUTRA

THE WAY BY WHICH SOUL UNITES WITH GOD

Sutra: - As the soul enables the eye to see and itself sees, so Hara enables the soul to know and itself knows. And this *Adwaitha* knowledge and undying Love will unite it to His Feet.

Commentary

The Sutra treats of the way by which the soul unites with the sacred foot of the Lord and consists of two arguments.

First Argument

Choornika: - *Hara* feels what the *Gnani* feels.

Varthikam: - It is proved that the Lord knows whatever the soul knows, as the soul cannot perceive anything, except with the aid of the Lord.

Udarana: - (*a*) As the soul becomes conscious of such objects only as it comes in contact with each of the senses separately, it cannot apprehend all the objects of the five senses at once, but apprehends them only one by one. But God sees and understands all things at once.

(*b*) When the soul unites itself to God and feels His *Arul*, God covers it with his Supreme Bliss and becomes one with it. Will He not know Himself who is understood by the soul through the intelligence of the soul?

Second Argument

Choornika: - If the *Gnani* has unfailing Love for Hara, he will become united to Him.

Varthikam: - It is shown that the soul unites with the Feet of the Lord, through unfailing Love, as He, dwelling in each man inseparably, metes out to each, according to his desert.

Udarana: - (*a*) The blind will only see darkness even in the presence of the Sun; just so, the soul entangled in *Pasa* cannot see *Isa* (though he is present in everything), Just as the Sun only opens the Lotus flower (when it is matured), so the darkness of those who understand Him by their Love will be removed by his *Arul*.

(*b*) As the Moon dispels the deep darkness, so God, who is connected with the soul from eternity, in His Love, removes the *Mala* of the soul and attracts it to Himself, just as the magnet attracts iron and brings it under control. While so operating, He incurs neither weariness nor change.

(*c*) When becoming one with God, if the soul perished, there will be nothing to unite with God, as it perishes. If it did not perish, it cannot become one with God. Just like the salt

Sivagnana Botham of Meykanda Deva

dissolved in water, the soul, after losing its *Mala*, unites itself to His Feet and becomes the servant of God (loses its individuality). Then it will have no darkness (no separation).

(*d*) Just as the rising Sun is enshrouded by the clouds and then appears, little by little, and when all the clouds are driven away, spreads its shining rays everywhere, so the soul's intelligence is enshrouded from eternity in *Mala* and brightens a little from its experience of the world; and getting rid of its *Mala* altogether, recovers its original intelligence and unites itself to the Feet of God.

NOTES

The last Sutra treated of *Pasatchaya* and the present one treats of attaining *Pathi Gnana* or *Anubava*. Leaving the case of those who postulate utter annihilation at this stage, in which case of course there could be no union (illustration 2c) and of those who postulate no *Anubava* at all, this Sutra points out how this *Anubava* arises. This *Anubava* is an *Anubava* of the soul in one sense, though not so in another sense. Here there is *Adwaitham* again. Dr. Bain instances the case of a man enjoying the keen pleasures of a warm bath as one of pure objective feeling or attitude; or as we would put it, it is the case of the man enjoying the pleasure of a cool bath during a hot day or what comes to the same thing, of the man who gets under the cool shelter of a spreading banyan tree (அடி நீழல்) after a hot and weary walk during the midday sun. Now substitute for the mind, the soul freed of *Pasa* and for the cool bath or cool shade, the Glorious Divine Light and its effulgence which permeates the soul through and through and diffuses all round it and completely bathes it in its *Arul*, and conceive then the soul's feeling of pleasure, its *Ananda*, Bliss. It is the soul that no doubt feels primarily but it ceases to live as such, and that very moment it becomes transformed into the Divine Feeling or *Anubava* itself. Just as the mind, when enjoying the pleasure of a bath, becomes purely objective, the soul becomes purely Divine when it feels His *Arul* and God covers it with Bliss (Illustration 1 b). As you feel the coolness of the bath or the shade more and more, your pleasure increases, so, as the soul feels His Arul more and more, its love of the Lord increases. So it is this (அயரா அன்பு) undying love, True Bhakti, that is the cause of the Soul's Supreme Happiness, Bliss and *Pathi Gnanam*. And in this *Adwaitha Anubava*, do we get the true definition of Love or Bhakti and see the profound meaning there is in the simple Mantra 'God is Love'; and now let us read again the Divine Mantra (which can bear repetition).

"அன்பும் சிவமும் இரண்டென்பர் அறிவிலார்
அன்பே சிவமாவ தாரு மறிந்திலார்
அன்பே சிவமாவ தாரு மறிந்தபின்
அன்பே சிவமா யமர்ந் திருப்பாரே."

Herein we have the true *Bhakti Marga*, or the true *Dasa Marga* which at the same time is seen to be the true *Gnana Marga*. Herein is seen no conflict between *Bhakti* and *Gnanam*. Yet how often do we see the followers of the so-called *Bhakti Marga* sneer at the follower of the so-called *Gnana Marga* and vice versa, when neither party have the least title to either name. The words, *Bhakta*, *Gnani* and *Mukta* are synonymous and the condition of the *Bhakta*

Sivagnana Botham of Meykanda Deva

involves and implies the passing through of the stages of *Sarya, Kriya* and *Yoga*, and it was a bad day for us when a wave of false devotion spread from the north to the south, thus undermining all principles of true progress by the practice of True *Tapas* and spreading instead, gross superstition and absurd rituals and ceremonies.

I cannot conclude this Sutra without pointing out an example of the exhibition of True *Bhakti* by a *Jivan Mukta* from the annals of the Saints recorded in our *Bhakta Vilasa*. Whom could I mean other than our Saint Kannappa?

"கண்ணப்பன் ஒப்பதோர் அன்பின்மை கண்டபின்"

Says our Saints Manika Vachaka, whose Divine words are sufficient to melt even the heart of stone to tears, and where he has chosen to praise, why need I refer to the host of other sages and writers who have loved to sing the praises of our Kannappa.

Says our Sri Sankaracharya also in his Sivanantha Lahiri.

"A pair of wooden shoes, worn out in paths becomes a bunch of holy grass to the person of *Siva*; the spitting of water raising the mouth, a holy bath; a mouthful of flesh partly eaten, a fresh oblation; and a forester, a great *Bhakta*; for nothing is impossible for *Bhakta*.

I dare not follow the subject any further.

Says, our Thayumanavar.

"அத்துவித அனுபவத்தை அனந்த மறை யின்ன மின்னம் அறியே மென்னும்."

(*d*) This is a most beautiful analogy and this being the last, sums up briefly the whole of the doctrine expounded in all the preceding chapters. It exhibits in clear and unmistakable language the passage of the soul through the *Kevala, Sakala,* and *Thurya Avasthas*. As the first part of the illustration stands, it would appear that it is the Sun that is enshrouded and that which appears little by little and then shines brightly. No, the language will be unmeaning from the stand point of the Sun. From its position it knows of no covering or shrouds or shining less or more. It is ever bright in itself. It is from the stand point of the human eye that all this language is employed. It is the eye that is enshrouded by the clouds and prevented therefore from seeing the glorious Sun and when the clouds are driven away little by little, the view of the Sun becomes better and better till at last, during the midday, the full refulgence of the glorious Sun is felt. The brevity of language, thus employed, in many of these analogies, have often misled many a thinker and we find the Hindu idealists use this very analogy to establish their theory of *Ekathma Vada*. As they put it, the clouds proceed from the Sun and then enshroud it, so Maya starts from Brahm and throws a Veil over it and then they proceed to build the whole fabric, in the first place an analogy to have any probative effect must be true in itself, i.e., the same sequence and consequence must exist in the thing compared as in the thing sought to be proved or inferred. Here, in the illustration, if it be true that the clouds proceed from the Sun, then we can say truly that the Maya proceeding from the Brahm serves to veil it. In no sense is the Sun the material cause of the cloud as the Brahm is said to be the

Sivagnana Botham of Meykanda Deva

material cause (*Upadanakarana*) of *Maya, Mulaprakriti, Jagat* or the universe. This essential condition failing, the whole superstructure must therefore tumble down. But let me elaborate the analogy properly and see what results it yields. Well, the Sun (Brahm) is not the material cause of the clouds (*Mulaprakriti*) but yet it is a cause of clouds. It is by the action of Sun's heat (Kriya Sakti) the clouds (*Mulaprakriti*) are formed out of water (*Maya*). Water itself cannot pass off into vapour and clouds but by the action of the Sun. So, Maya cannot evolve into Jagat or the universe but for the *Kriya Sakti* of the Lord. No doubt, when the clouds are formed by the action of the Sun, these clouds do enshroud, well, not the Sun but the human eye. The very instant you use the word shrouding or veiling, you imply a third thing placed on the other side of the veil. The human eye can no more be derived from the Sun than the soul or human monad from Brahm. Though in either case the eye or the soul can only see or know but with the dim or full light of the Sun or God, Brahm. The greater or less dimness is caused by the thickness or lightness of the clouds or Maya coating. And as the eye and the Sun approximate nearer and nearer, the clouds are dissipated away, and so, as the soul comes nearest to God, *Maya* vanishes.

Take another example of Analogy used by the same school of thinkers; and this is a most favorite one with them. It is the simile of the Sun shining in many pots of water, serving to illustrate the principle that the souls are derived from God. Here the resemblances are not exact and the consequence does not follow. In the one case we have only Brahm from which we have got to derive many souls. On the other hand, we have on Sun and many pots which are also filled with water to reproduce not many Suns but merely the shadow or reflection of the Sun. Neither is the shadow the same as the Sun nor are the pots and water derived from the Sun. but let us view the analogy from another point and see how pregnant it is. The Sun is Brahm, the pot is Maya or Pasa binding the naturally expansive water or the soul. And the reflection of the Sun is God's presence in Man and the Sun's reflection or light passes through the water and lies on it and yet is not contaminated nor touched by it. So God being a *Gnana Swarupi*, chit or Mahachaitanyam, though in contact with the world and souls, are not tainted by it and feels no weariness nor change (illustration 2b). And the breaking of the pot, Pasatchaya, releases the water from its confined condition and it vanishes into invisible vapour before the heat of the Sun. (*Arul* of God). In the same way, almost every analogy employed by the Hindu idealists can be easily shown to falsify their own position and support the position herein established.

Analogy, I may say is largely used in this work as a method of proof, as any other kind of proof is hardly possible when dealing with the nature of the very ultimate of all existences. The conjunction of the mind and body, it is admitted, is a unique phenomenon in nature. Its conjunction cannot be proved, being the very ultimate of all facts; and the position can only be proved or illustrated by various analogies, say for instance, the analogy of vowels and consonants (Vide Sutra No. 2). So we pass on from this conjunction of mind and body to that of Soul and mind and to that of Brahm or God and Soul, and the unions in all these cases are analogous.

Sivagnana Botham of Meykanda Deva

XII - TWELFTH SUTRA

ON THE MODE OF WORSHIP OF GOD WHO SURPASSES POWERS OF THOUGHT AND SPEECH

Sutra: - Let the *Jivatma*, after washing off its *Mala* which separates it from the strong Lotus feet of the Lord and mixing in the society of *Bhaktas* (*Jivan Muktas*) whose souls abound with Love, having lost dark ignorance, contemplate their Forms and the Forms in the temples as His Form.

Commentary

This treats of the mode of finding and worshipping the *Pathi* who cannot be seen and thought of, and consists of four arguments.

First Argument

Choornika. – Get rid of the three *Malas*.

Varthikam: - It is pointed out that the three *Malas* should be got rid of, as they will only beget ignorance or evil, instead of wisdom.

Udarana: - Let the true *Gnani* leave alone the three *Malas*, namely, *Karma*, which is the effect and cause of good and bad acts; *Maya*, from which is developed the *tatwas* from earth to motive; and *Anava*, which begets *Ahankara*, as these will harm him.

Second Argument

Choornika: - Join the Society of *Sivagnanis*.

Varthikam: - It is pointed out that the Society of *Sivabhakthas* should be sought, as others will only impart evil.

Udarana: - The *Karma* will not affect the true *Gnani* who leaving the Society of ignoble persons (who forget themselves and suffer in *Mala*), join the Society of Bhakthas and understand with the Light of God.

Third Argument

Choornika: - Worship *Sivagnanis* and *Siva Linga* as *Siva*.

Varthikam: - It is enjoined that the forms if *Bhakthas* and the *Siva Linga* should be worshipped as *Parameshwara* as He shines brightly in these Forms, though He is present in everything.

Udarana: - (*a*) The Lord *Pathi* wishing that all should understand Him gives His Form to His *Bhakthas* who desire to know Him and makes them know Himself and keeps them in

Sivagnana Botham of Meykanda Deva

His own self and makes Himself visible, as butter in curds. To those entangled in *Pasa*, He is invisible as is butter in milk.

(*b*) As the fire appears distinct from the pieces of wood rubbed together, So the Lord who exists in all visible forms, and yet is different from them, will be present in a visible form composed of *Mantra*. To those who can view the Form itself as God, will He not appear as that Form itself.

Fourth Argument

Choornika: - Cease not to so worship Him.

Varthikam: - The worship of Him in these Forms is enjoined, as though these Forms are not Himself, yet He is in these Forms; just as man, though constituted of muscles, bones, nerves, &c., yet is neither muscles nor bones, &c.

Udarana: - (*a*) To the *Seer*, God is neither different from all things, nor is He one with them, nor one and different from them. He is in the general *Adwaitha* relation with them, and everything is His form; and yet let the *Adwaithi* worship the Form which excites his Love most.

(*b*) As acts only lead to ignorance unless the previous *Karma* is removed, *Gnanam* will not rise. This *Karma* will cease and Gnanam will rise when the Society of Gnanis is sought and they are worshipped. Therefore worship them in all Love.

(*c*) To forget the Lord, who made him know himself and transformed him like unto Himself, is an inexcusable sin. Though he, who was always a servant, is now transformed like unto Himself, yet he continues to be only His servant. Hence his strength consists in the worship.

(*d*) O thou student of *Saiva Siddhanta*, those who have one and two mala, namely, *Vignanakalars* and *Pralayakalars*, lose their mortal nature and attain the Divine knowledge, by respectively being taught intuitively by the innate God, and by being purified by the eye &c., of the Divine Guru. This book is intended to be taught to *Sakalars* who have three Malas by their Supreme Guru.

NOTES

In Sivagnana Siddhi, the purport of this Sutra is given as *Adiavar Lakshana* or *Bhakta Lakshana*. The *Jivan Mukta*, even after he has obtained the *Anubuthi* as described in the last Sutra, cannot afford to indulge in Karmic acts so long as he is encased in the flesh. There is no playing with fire. If he does, he is sure to be brought back again into the Cycle of Karmic evolution. Hence the caution conveyed in the first argument, but if he should do anything or wish to do anything, let him join the Society of Bhaktas, and avoid the Society of sinners. He is also directed to love them and worship their forms and the forms in the temple. In this mode of worship, is pointed out the way for other mortals, of worship of God who surpasses powers of thought and speech. In the preceding pages, I have pointed out why it is not possible to know God. Yet in our own heart of hearts, we yearn to worship and glorify Him, and this necessity

Sivagnana Botham of Meykanda Deva

is also provided for. The principle of it is found in the fact that God is Omnipresent and is one with or in Adwaitha relation with everything, animate and inanimate. We must worship Him as one of these. Hence it is, in the Veda, in *Sri Rudram*, God is addressed by naming every object of creation. The Gnani who sees the objects, does not see them though, buy only God's presence. However for mortals, they have got a choice. God, though He is present in everything, is non-apparent as the ghee in the milk. But there are forms, in which we can feel His Presence more apparently like the butter in the curds.

"விறகிற்றீயினன் பாலிற் படுநெய் போல்
மறைய நின்றனன் மாமணிச் சோதியான்
உறவு கோல் நட்டு உணர்வு கயிற்றினாள்
முறுக வாங்கிக் கடையமுன் னீற்குமே."

"Like the fire latent in wood and the ghee latent in milk, the *Great Jodhi* (Light) is non-apparent. But with the churner of Love and the rope of knowledge, on churns the milk or rubs the firewood, butter or fire will become apparent."

So, it is in the body of Bhaktas that God's Presence is a living Presence, and it is by reason of this, the divine word that "Ye are the Temple of God," is pre-eminently true. So when we want to worship Him, we must worship Him in the Bhakta. But it is not the whole truth to say that we are alone the Temples of God. He is everywhere and especially in forms which excite our Love most (4a). This is the general rule for all. It does not matter what form people choose, provided it is that which excite their Love most. Passing beyond this law, is the principle that all the forms in the temples are what are said to be *Mantra Swarupam*. The Form adopted is not an unmeaning stock or stone but one full of meaning and of the Divine Idea. I have elsewhere enlarged upon this subject, and it may be here sufficient to remark that mantrams are symbolic representations of the Deity by the ear and when the same are converted into symbols of the eye, we get the Forms in our temples. (3b) let the ignorant, therefore, not sneer at our temples. The various cautions conveyed in the arguments and illustrations of this very sutra, not to mistake the symbol for the truth, and not to suppose that God is only present in these Forms, will clear up all doubts that may exist in the matter. Then, again, of all the Forms, that are to be met with in our temples, from *Gouri Shanker* (Mt Everest) to Cape Comorin and beyond, and from the Caves of Elephanta to Mahabalipuram, the form of the Linga is the most universal and frequent; and not only so, it is, in fact, the most ancient form of worship. It may be noticed that the Linga For of worship is the one most met with in the pages of the Mahabharatha; for instance, see the conversation which takes place between Vyasa and Ashwathama after the latter was defeated by Arjuna, in which Vyasa points out that the real cause of superiority in Arjuna, consisted in his worshipping the Linga Form of Siva, whereas Ashwathama worshipped a Personal Form of Siva. But it is not only in the pages of Mahabharatha and Ramayana that this form of worship is met with, but hundreds of passages from the Veda and Upanishads may be quoted to prove the worship. The reader is further cautioned not to mistake the *Linga* for any phallic symbol, as is ignorantly supposed. See the pages of 'the Secret Doctrine' for an explanation of the '*Lipika*,' which almost applies to the *Linga*.

Sivagnana Botham of Meykanda Deva

Cf. The words of the Great Poet:

"There was a time when meadow, grove, and stream,
　　The earth, and every common object,
　　　　To me did seem,
　　Apparell'd in Celestial light,
The Glory and the freshness of a dream."

    This is as regards the recollections of the child; but scientists may or may not agree with the poet, if the child does possess any thoughts at all at the time. The poet had yet to rise to the thought that to the True *Bhakta* or *Gnani* the earth and every common object will appear apparelled in celestial light; and more, the earthly aspect will altogether vanish before him and the Divine Presence alone will be felt.

Sivagnana Botham of Meykanda Deva

IN PRAISE OF MEYKANDA DEVA

The Saint *Meykanda Deva* has translated together with reasons and illustrations for the benefit of mankind, the great Sivagnana Botham which was graciously given out by Nandi at the earnest entreaties of my master *Sanatkumara*.

Let me worship the teacher who has translated, in Tamil, *Sivagnana Botham* which, like the mirror reflecting a great mountain, contains in itself all the truths contained in all the learned Shastras.

Sivagnana Botham of Meykanda Deva

GLOSSARY

Abeda	---	One-ness; one; not different.
Abhava	---	A term used in Logic to denote one of the even categories, meaning non-existence.
Achalam	---	Immovable; permanent.
Achit	---	Non-intelligent; non-Ego; matter; Asat.
Adikarana	---	A complete argument dealing with one question a thesis.
Adisakti	---	The Original Divine Power or Light identified with the Divine Light of Gayatri.
Adisukshuma	---	Least of the least; most subtle.
Adwaitha	---	Non-dualism.
Agama	---	The revealed word, one of the 28 books, ascribed to God, Siva.
Agama Pramana	---	One of the four proofs employed by Hindu Logicians, meaning the Highest authority or word of God, Sabda Pramana, Sruthi Pramana.
Agna	---	Authority.
Agna Sakti	---	The Divine Power.
Agnanam	---	Ignorance.
Ahadyanam	---	Inner worship; esoteric worship; true worship.
Ahankara	---	One of the four Andakaranas; Pride of self; self-knowledge.
Akamia Karma	---	See under Karma.
Akas	---	The highest of the five elements; Ether.
Anava	---	See under Pasa.
Andakarana	---	A generic name to denote all the four internal senses, Manas, Bhuddhi, Chittam and Ahankara.
Ananda	---	Bliss; Happiness.
Anekesvara Vadi	---	The School of Thinkers who hold that there are many Gods.

Sivagnana Botham of Meykanda Deva

Anumana	---	Inference; one of the four proofs of Hindu Logicians.
Anu	---	An atom; very small Soul.
Anubhava	---	Experience.
Anubhuthi	---	Experience.
Arivu	---	Intelligence; Soul.
Arul	---	Grace; Divine Grace.
Arul Sakti	---	The Power of Divine Grace.
Asat	---	Non-ego; matter, other than Sat; Achit, other than Souls, and God.
Atma	---	This word is invariably used to denote the Soul, in all Siddhanta works; In Vedanta works, this word is used to denote the Soul, Jivatma, and God, Paramatma.
Avastha	---	One of the conditions or states of the Soul's existence.
Jagra avastha	---	Waking state.
Swapna avastha	---	Dreaming state.
Sushupthi avastha	---	State of dead sleep.
Thuriya avastha	---	State of the Soul breathing in bodies, in which consciousness is not yet developed.
Kevala avastha	---	The avastha named last is Kevala Avastha. The other four avasthas constitute *Sakala avastha*. The state of the Jivanmukta is the *Sutta avastha*.
Avatar	---	Incarnation.
Aviddhei	---	Ignorance.
Bandham	---	Bond; fetters.
Mala Bandham	---	Bond of ignorance and of matter.
Bavana	---	Imagining; thinking of something else as known.
Soham bavana	---	Imagining God as one-self.
Bhakti	---	Love of God; Devotion.

Sivagnana Botham of Meykanda Deva

Betham	---	Difference; Duality.
Beethabetham	---	Being non-dual and dual.
Brahm	---	(Neuter Gender); (Literally) means Great; Supreme Being; The Omnipresent Being.
Brahma	---	(Masculine Gender) one of the Hindu Trinity regarded as the author of creation; according to the view of the Siddhantin, he is regarded as a mortal as well as the other two of the Trinity.
Bhoga	---	Enjoyment.
Bhouddam	---	Buddhism, exoteric as it is now called, denying the existence of the Soul and God, and proclaiming the supremacy of the human Reason or Buddhi alone.
Buddhi	---	Reason; one of the four Andakaranas.
Buvana	---	The whole material universe.
Chaitanyam	---	Intelligence.
Maha Chaitanyam	---	Supreme Intelligence.
Chit	---	Intelligence.
Chit Sakti	---	Divine Intelligence or Energy; Gnana Sakti.
Chittam	---	Sense of Perception; one of the four Andakaranas.
Choornika	---	A brief abstract; a style of expression.
Dwaitham	---	Dualism.
Ekam	---	One.
Ekatma Vadam	---	Monism; the theory according to which there is only one Intelligent entity and that there are no such entities as Souls or matter; the theory of Idealism.
Guru	---	(Literally) The dispeller of darkness; The teacher who removes the ignorance of his pupil.
Sat Guru or Sarguru	---	The Divine Teacher, who by His Grace, removes the fetters of man.
Gnanam	---	Intelligence; knowledge; wisdom.
Gnana Sakti	---	The Divine Intelligence.

Sivagnana Botham of Meykanda Deva

Gneya	---	Knowable.
Gnathru	---	The Knower.
Hara	---	The Supreme Energy; God; Siva; Iswara.
Hetu	---	The reason; one of the propositions in the Syllogism of the Hindu Logician.
Homam	---	Sacrifice.
Isa	---	Hara; Siva; God; Brahm.
Isvara	---	This word as used by Siddhantins is Synonymous with Brahm but as used by Sri Sankaracharya, it means the Lower Brahm and the distinction of Higher and Lower Brahm finds no place in the Siddhanta School.
Indriya	---	Sensory organ.
Jagat	---	The universe; the world; matter.
Jagra avastha	---	See Avastha.
Jiva	---	The Soul; the embodied Soul.
Jivan Mukta	---	The person who has obtained liberation or final bliss even as he is in the human body. He can never be reborn in the flesh. The so-called Mahatmas are not Jivan Muktas but mortals enjoying a higher plane of existence. A Christ or a Buddha, may become a Jivan Mukta and if it is said of them that they are reborn in the flesh at different times, they are not Muktas but only mortals.
Jothi	---	Light.
Kalpa	---	Periodic evolution.
Karma	---	One of the three Bandas or Mala or Pasa which fetters the Soul. The sum total of human action, involved as cause and effect, producing pleasure and pain and causing rebirths.
Praraptha	---	Fruits of previous Karma eaten in the present life.
Akamia	---	Such seeds when sown in the next life become Sangchitham.
Karana	---	A sense organ, whether external or internal.
Karana	---	Cause.
Nimitha	---	Efficient cause.

Sivagnana Botham of Meykanda Deva

Upathana	---	Material cause.
Thunai or Sahakari	---	Instrumental Cause.
Karana Sarira	---	See Sarira.
Karta	---	Creator; the Lord; God.
Kevala avastha	---	See Avastha.
Kriya	---	Action, ritual or ceremonial. The second of the four Pathams or modes or Sadana for attaining Moksha.
Kriya Sakti	---	The Divine Energy. God as conceived as the author of evolution.
Lokayatha	---	The materialist; the atheist.
Mala	---	Impurity; Impurity of the Soul; the coverings or fetters of the Soul.
Maya	---	(Literally). That which is evolved and resolved; matter; cosmic matter; no ego; object. It does not mean Mitya or delusion or illusion. I find the word invariably so translated in all the existing translations of Sanskrit works into English. This is forcing into the word the views of a particular school of Philosophers, namely the Hindu Idealists.
Anava	---	Agnana; Ignorance, the Soul's inherent impurity or imperfection.
Karma	---	See Karma above.
Manas	---	The faculty of the mind which is exercised immediately after a perception. One of the four Andakaranas.
Mantra	---	A Vedic Hymn; any prayer or sacred or mystic word recited or contemplated in Divine worship.
Mayavadam	---	Idealism. The doctrine that regards the Souls and the material universe as non-existent, a mere myth, a delusion or illusion. The Saiva, Ramanuja, and Madhwa are all agreed in applying the term to denote the Hindu Idealist, though the Hindu Idealist does not relish the term and the usage itself is very old. The same as Ekatmavadam.
Mayavadi	---	An Idealist.

Sivagnana Botham of Meykanda Deva

Mitya	---	Illusion or delusion. Could this word have been confounded with Maya?
Mukta	---	The finally emancipated and beatified Soul. (Lit:) freed.
Mukti	---	Emancipation from Pasa or Mala Bandha and attaining Bliss or Anantha Anubhava.
Moksha	---	Same as Mukti.
Mulaprakriti	---	Same as Maya; undifferentiated cosmic matter.
Nasthikam	---	Atheism.
Natham	---	The sound of Pranava. The deity as representing the sound of the Pranava; God, as present in the universe, when at the very beginning of evolution, the great Sound or Subdam or Natham bursts forth; cosmic matter in the state of Sound.
Nimitta Karana	---	See Karana.
Nirvikari	---	The unchangeable.
Nirmala or Ninmalaa	---	The Perfect Being; The Pure Being.
Padartha	---	An entity or category.
Panchatchara	---	The Mystic Mantra, formed out of Pranava and used by Saivas in Divine contemplation.
Papam	---	Sin or Sinful acts; acts tending to cause pain to sentient beings.
Paripooranam	---	Omnipresence.
Paraprayoganam	---	The good of others; Altruistic Acts.
Pasa	---	A bond or fetters of impurity or darkness; same as Mala; see Mala.
Pasu	---	Soul; Atma.
Pathi	---	The Lord; God; Siva.
Pathignana	---	Sivagnana.
Pillaiyar	---	The Divine Child; God Ganesha.
Pillaiyar Shuli	---	The Symbol of Ganesha; Pranava.
Prakasa	---	Light.
Pramana	---	Mode of Proof; Proof.
Agama Pramana	---	Proof or a thing by means of God' word or of a trustworthy Authority.

Sivagnana Botham of Meykanda Deva

Anumana Pramana---		Proof of Inference.
Prathiaksha Pramana---		Proof by observation.
Upamana Pramana---		Proof by analogy.
Prapancha	---	The universe; Jagat; the seen universe.
Pranavayu	---	The breath or Life as distinct from the Soul. Yet, ludicrously enough some Missionaries and Oriental Scholars think that we mistake the breath for the Soul and that we have no idea of the Soul!
Praraptha Karma	---	See Karma.
Pralaya Kalars	---	Souls with fetters of Karma Mala and Anava Mala.
Puja	---	Worship; contemplation.
Purusha	---	The Soul.
Sabda Brahm	---	Same as Natha Brahm; God, as represented in Mantric form audible to the ear.
Sadana	---	Mode or way of attaining some end. The practices, physical and otherwise for emancipating one-self, from Pasa and attaining Bliss.
Sarya	---	Devotional practices, altruistic in their nature.
Kriya	---	Religious rituals and worship of God.
Yoga	---	Psychical Practices, required for contemplation of God.
Gnana	---	Attaining the knowledge of God.
Sadasivam	---	Same as Siva Sat or Sat Chit, God manifest to the World as Divine Energy (Kriya) and Supreme Intelligence (Gnana). The Hindu Trinity merely represents God's Energy or Kriya aspect, and not His Gnana aspect.
Sahakari	---	See Karana.
Sakti	---	Divine Power.
Ichcha Sakti	---	Divine Will.
Kriya Sakti	---	Divine Energy.
Jnana Sakti	---	Divine Intelligence.
Sakalar	---	Souls of the last order possessing all the three Mala Banthams, and includes, all sentient beings and Devas.

Sivagnana Botham of Meykanda Deva

Samavaya	---	One of the seven categories of the Hindu Logicians. Inseparable co-inheritance of attributes.
Samharam	---	Decay; Reabsorption; Resolution; Dissolution.
Sankara	---	The Doer of Good; God; Siva.
Sarguru or Satguru	---	The True Teacher; the Divine Teacher; see Guru.
Sarguru Darshan	---	The sight of the Divine Guru.
Sarira	---	Body.
Sthula Sarira	---	The body of the soul in the waking state or Jagra avastha.
Sukshuma or *Linga Sarira*	---	The body of the soul in the Swapna avastha or Dream condition.
Karana Sarira	---	The body in profound sleep and in two other higher avasthas.
Sat	---	The Truth; That which is permanent; God regarded as Himself and not as manifest to the world.
Sat Chit	---	Same as Sadasivam or Siva Sat. God regarded as Sat when it is not manifest to the World and as Chit when it is manifest to the World.
Satchidananda	---	God when known by the Mukta; when God appears as Love.
Siddhantam	---	The True End; the Saiva Adwaitha Philosophy.
Siddhantin	---	A Saiva; a follower of the above school.
Siva	---	Brahm; God and not one of the Trinity.
Sivoham	---	Same as Soham.
Sivagnanam	---	See Pathi Gnanam.
Sivagnana Siddhi	---	The second of the 14 Siddhanta Sastras and the largest and most comprehensive work of the series.
Soham	---	It is I; God is myself; One of the Sadanas required for elevating the Soul to the Presence of God; used also as Hara.
Swarupam	---	Form.
Srishti	---	Creation; origination.
Sthithi	---	Development; sustentation.

Sivagnana Botham of Meykanda Deva

Sunyam	---	Non-apparent, as when the object vanishes in pure subjective mood. It does not mean non-existence or nothing.
Sushupthi	---	See Avastha.
Swathanthram	---	A free right.
Swaprayojanam	---	Selfish end; one's own good.
Tanu	---	Animal Body.
Tapas	---	Sarya, Kriya and Yoga; Religious and ascetic practices; Devotion.
Tapoloka	---	Heavens; conditions or states of the Souls undergoing rest after death, the condition being pleasurable.
Tatparam	---	Supreme Lord; of all.
Tatwas	---	Component parts of the body and Soul.
Teganmavadi	---	Materialist; those who, deny the existence of a mind and Soul.
Thripadartha	---	The three entities, postulated by Saivas, and Vaishnavas.
Turiya	---	See Avasthas.
Turiyatheetha	---	See Avasthas.
Udarana	---	An analogy; illustration or Upamana.
Upamana	---	Same as Udarana.
Upamana Poli	---	False analogy.
Upadana Karana	---	See Karana.
Vartikam	---	A concise explanatory note.
Vasana Mala	---	Evil of association, or habit.
Vishnu	---	In Siddhanta Philosophy, Vishnu is one of the Trinity, and does not represent the Thuriya Padartha, the Supreme Brahm. It represents Mulaprakriti Tatwa. He is capable of Avatars and as such included among the Sakalars. It is a personal God and is regarded as an anthromorphic representation.
Vinthu	---	The form of Pranava.
Vijnanakalar	---	The highest of the three order of Souls. They have only Anava Mala.

Sivagnana Botham of Meykanda Deva

Visishtadwaitam	---	Qualified non-dualism.
Vyapaka	---	All container.
Vyappiya	---	The contained.
Vyapti	---	Associated with the contained.
Yoga	---	Psychical practices used as aids to Divine contemplation and for acquiring spiritual power.

www.ingramcontent.com/pod-product-compliance
Lightning Source LLC
Chambersburg PA
CBHW020157170426
43199CB00010B/1087